About This Book

The book delves into the systemic flaws present in the criminal justice system and shines a
light on the unjust practices within the prison system. It meticulously unpacks the
conditions under which inmates are effectively coerced into laboring under harsh and
exploitative circumstances, essentially operating as a modern-day slave labor force.
Furthermore, it discusses the process by which the goods produced by these inmates are
distributed and sold in the broader market, leading to the financialization of prisons and
their subsequent listing on the stock exchange. The text raises profound concerns about
the intricate web of individuals within the legal system, encompassing lawyers, judges,
prosecutors, congressmen, senators, and other law enforcement officials who invest in
correctional facilities and derive financial gain from the labor of incarcerated individuals.
This pervasive conflict of interest may, alarmingly, result in the unjust incarceration of
individuals solely to bolster production and maximize profits, irrespective of their guilt or
innocence

Dr. R. Phillips is a traditional cowboy and southern gentleman known for his signature Black Stetson Cowboy hat. His Christian faith and moral values, instilled by his loving parents, shape his character. With a passion for research and sharing knowledge, he has delivered lectures and sermons across the United States. After completing his academic pursuits, he became a Baptist minister and obtained a master's degree in biblical archaeology and a doctorate in divinity. He has actively championed human rights, particularly those of inmates, and is working on several forthcoming books to contribute positively to society.

CONVICTING FOR PROFITS

The Priority of Filling Prisons over Justice for the Innocent

DR. ROBERT PHILLIPS

C.O.L.T. MINISTRIES

CONVICTING FOR PROFITS

Contents

CONCLUSION

I DEDICATE THIS BOOK TO MY PARENTS, RONALD AND PATRICIA PHILLIPS. THEIR LOVE AND SUPPORT HAVE SHAPED ME INTO WHO I AM TODAY. THEY HAVE BEEN THERE FOR ME THROUGH THICK AND THIN, AND I AM FOREVER GRATEFUL FOR THEIR UNWAVERING ENCOURAGEMENT. THANK YOU BOTH, I LOVE YOU VERY MUCH.

TO MY MOM AND DAD,

YOUR EVER-GRATEFUL SON,

ROBERT

Convicting for Profits:

THE PRIORITY OF FILLING PRISONS OVER JUSTICE FOR THE INNOCENT

INTRODUCTION

Since the inception of the Prison Industrial Complex (PIC), there have been crucial and defining moments in terms of legislative action that have ultimately resulted in a significant rise in the utilization of prisons and the imprisonment of countless innocent individuals. Among the myriad turning points, one that stands out as particularly noteworthy and deserving of our attention is the enactment of the 1996 Prison Litigation Reform Act (PLRA). This Act, commonly called the PLRA, effectively restricts prisoners from filing claims for judicial relief about prison conditions unless they have thoroughly exhausted all available administrative remedies. While on the surface, this may not seem like a significant setback in the quest for justice when it comes to cases of wrongful imprisonment and the unjust detention of the innocent, one must delve deeper to understand the full extent and implications of this legislation.

The ramifications of the PLRA are profound and extend far beyond what meets the eye. By forcing prisoners to navigate a labyrinthine administrative process before they can seek legal redress regarding their inhumane and unjust treatment within the prison system, the PLRA essentially erects insurmountable barriers for those wrongfully incarcerated. It places a burden upon burden on the already burdened, leaving the innocent languishing in a seemingly endless cycle of bureaucracy, all while administrators and authorities enjoy the luxury of time ticking away. Consequently, this creates an inherently unequal and imbalanced battle between the prisoners, who must serve their sentence in perpetuity, and a system that seems determined to ensure that they never truly have their day in court.

However, it is not just the PLRA that contributes to the quagmire of wrongful imprisonment; it is also the convergence of federal funding and legislative measures that compound the issue, exacerbating this phenomenon. A glaring example lies in the unparalleled increase of federal funding, a staggering 500% surge, which was injected into the criminal justice system through the Anti-Terrorism and Effective Death Penalty Act (ATEDPA) and the Innocence Protection Act (IPA). These acts, purportedly initiated to combat terrorism and safeguard the innocent, ironically end up perpetuating a broken system and greasing the wheels of injustice.

By funneling substantial financial resources to the states, the ATEDPA and the IPA inadvertently create an environment conducive to expedited convictions and the relentless perpetuation of wrongful imprisonments. Rather than functioning as measures to protect the innocent and ensure a fair and just justice system, these acts inadvertently serve as catalysts for hasty and erroneous verdicts, leading to the imprisonment of countless innocent individuals who find themselves entangled in the machinery of a flawed and prejudiced system.

In conclusion, the confluence of the PLRA with the increased federal funding via the ATEDPA and the IPA has irrevocably tilted the scales of justice in favor of wrongful imprisonment and the detention of the innocent. The interconnectedness of these legislative actions has paved the way for a system that systematically relegates the rights and well-being of prisoners to a secondary position, perpetuating an atmosphere of oppression, injustice, and despair. We must confront and address these critical junctures head-on if we are to reclaim the fundamental principles of fairness, justice, and humanity in our criminal justice system. (Foss, 2023)(Reilly, 2020)

I

The Profit motive in Prison Industry

Prison Industrial Complex (PIC) is a highly contentious and thought-provoking term that is widely employed to attribute the staggering and alarming growth of the inmate population in the United States to the profound and perplexing political influence exerted by private prison companies and an intricate network of businesses that incessantly supply an array of goods and indispensable services to the sprawling and intricate government prison agencies, encompassing a multifaceted conglomerate that casts a pervasive and indelible shadow on the fabric of the nation's criminal justice system.

It is essential to comprehend that the term PIC encapsulates a multifaceted web of interdependencies and intricate dynamics, predominantly centered around the profound and unprecedented economic influence held by private prison companies over the domains of criminal justice, ultimately culminating in a staggering and unsettling increase in the number of individuals languishing behind bars, bereft of their freedom and stripped of their fundamental human rights.

Within the intricate complexities of the PIC, one of the most widely recognized and comprehended facets pertains to the private contracting arrangements orchestrated by these prison enterprises, wherein prisoners are systematically exploited and coerced into servitude, with their labor being relentlessly exploited to provide a vast array of goods and indispensable services, all the while being subjected to deplorable conditions and nominal remuneration that utterly pales in comparison to the worth of their labor.

It is crucial to underscore that the prison labor industry relies inexorably on a persistent and long-term source of dirt-cheap labor to thrive and achieve continued success. In a somewhat disconcerting turn of events, it becomes apparent that the state, propelled by a prevailing and fervent inclination to adopt draconian and stringent "get tough on crime" policies, has emerged as a veritable and dependable provider of such an abundant and continuous supply of cheap labor, thereby perpetuating a self-perpetuating cycle of inherent human rights abuses and systemic oppression within the vast confines of the infamous PIC. (Appleman, 2022)Reiman and Leighton, 2020)

Currently, the United States stands as the undeniable global leader in incarceration rates. It is truly astounding that the U.S. has imprisoned an unprecedented number of individuals, surpassing any other country in the world. To put this staggering reality into perspective, the U.S. has locked up half a million more people than China, a country with a population five times larger than that of the United States. The statistics, which reveal this grossly disproportionate truth, show that the declared number of public and private prisons is capable of housing an estimated 1.6 million inmates. However, upon closer examination of this data, a startling revelation emerges: for the prison industry to continue thriving, a more significant influx of inmates is essential despite the dubious prospect of increased crime.

This leaves us with corrupt or mistaken convictions as the seemingly viable solution to fueling the industry's exponential growth. Furthermore, it is alarmingly plausible that allowing corporations to advocate for longer sentences would serve as the second option to accommodate an ever-growing number of inmates, thereby enhancing the profitability per incarcerated individual. With nefarious legislation like the abhorrent "three strikes law" lurking in the shadows, the possibility of doling out life sentences for offenses that would typically warrant a minor reprimand becomes a chilling reality. This could incentivize the perpetuation of criminal activities to sustain an alarmingly high prison population artificially.

The increased presence of high-security risk inmates, combined with longer sentences, seems to bolster private corporations' financial gains, albeit at a grave cost. This bleak reality not only poses an unparalleled threat to innocent individuals who might fall victim to harm at the hands of seasoned criminals but also effectively undermines the very foundation of justice and fairness we should uphold. It is disheartening and profoundly unsettling to acknowledge that in the relentless pursuit of maximizing profits, the equation becomes ruthless: more inmates equate to more significant financial gains.

Under this scheme, where monetary considerations outweigh the inherent value of human life, it is no surprise that minimizing operating costs becomes the modus operandi. Tragically, history has demonstrated time and time again that ministries of justice have consistently struggled with systemic mismanagement of funds. Consequently, any efforts to curtail expenditures would inevitably birth devastating consequences borne by the most vulnerable: the innocent individuals whose unjust incarceration would serve as a methodical sacrifice at the altar of corporate greed. (Young, 2020)

Similar to any corporation, a prison's primary objective is to generate profit. To achieve this goal, prisons must maintain full occupancy. Two main strategies are used to achieve this profitability and secure financial success for the institution. The first method involves increasing the number of incarcerated individuals within the facility, a common approach many correctional institutions adopt. Conversely, the second method emphasizes cost efficiency, as prisons aim to minimize daily operational expenses.

Unfortunately, this relentless pursuit of profit often results in a perversion of justice within the criminal justice system. Consequently, innocent individuals are wrongfully convicted and, in extreme cases, subjected to capital punishment for crimes they did not commit. This egregious miscarriage of justice not only tarnishes the integrity of the legal system but also inflicts immeasurable suffering upon innocent victims and their families. This injustice's far-reaching and deeply troubling consequences erode public trust and undermine the foundation of a fair and just society. We must address and rectify these systemic issues to safeguard innocent lives and uphold the principles of justice and fairness that form the bedrock of our society. (Raher, 2020)(Wooldredge, 2020)

The Impact on the Criminal Justice System The insatiable pursuit of profit by private prison companies is strikingly similar to that of any typical corporation. These companies relentlessly strive for financial gain by implementing many strategies, all aimed at increasing their profits and ensnaring a more significant number of individuals within the confines of their prisons. These strategies entail exerting considerable influence over both the State and Federal Government through intense lobbying efforts and actively encouraging the creation of laws that impose substantially harsher prison sentences. Furthermore, private prison companies work tirelessly to instill fear among the public, perpetuating the belief that crime rates are rapidly escalating. They also allocate significant resources to politicians who adopt a more stringent "tough on crime" stance, effectively replacing those perceived as "soft on crime."

The culmination of these endeavors perpetuates a system that is riddled with numerous human rights violations as the prison industrial complex thrives, preying on communities that the criminal justice system has shattered. The legislation fervently advocated by the private prison industry and other organizations championing tough-on-crime initiatives has drastically transformed the justice system over the past two to three decades. Shockingly, despite stable crime rates in the United States, the number of individuals behind bars has skyrocketed from approximately 300,000 to a staggering 2.2 million within just thirty years.

This alarming escalation in the prison population can largely be attributed to legislation endorsing severe penalties for drug-related offenses. However, it is crucial to note that while the majority of drug offenders are White, African Americans and Latinos have been disproportionately targeted within the United States, facing heightened arrest rates and prosecution.

The devastating consequences of the War on Drugs have resulted in an egregiously imbalanced number of minorities being incarcerated for such offenses. Moreover, these imprisoned individuals, who are already disadvantaged by the system, are ruthlessly denied even the most basic human rights and often become unwitting subjects of pharmaceutical experiments. The implications of these new medications on prisoners' health and well-being have been egregiously overlooked, casting doubt on the seriousness with which their effects have been considered.

The legislative changes and excessively punitive sentences propagated by the private prison industry have undeniably benefited a select few, namely those who own and operate the prisons. However, the victims of this deeply flawed system of human rights abuses extend beyond the incarcerated individuals in the United States. With the prevailing trend of increased spending on prisons and the disturbing absence of substantial legislation dedicated to rehabilitating criminals and ex-convicts, the United States has now arrived at a critical juncture where the cost of maintaining the justice system significantly outweighs the associated benefits. Furthermore, when considering that taxpayers bear an exorbitant average price of $29,000 per year to house just one prisoner, it becomes glaringly evident who bears the overwhelming financial burden in this profoundly unjust system.

2

Historical Background and Context

Understanding the historical background is crucial when attempting to grasp the intricate nature of the prison-industrial complex. Although prisons have been a fixture in society for a long time, the pervasive practice of imprisoning individuals for extended periods is relatively new in the annals of the United States.

Delving into the past offers valuable insight, revealing that between 1925 and 1975, the imprisonment rate remained remarkably stable, establishing a sense of balance. Nevertheless, the transformative year of 1975 became a defining moment as the incarceration rate initiated an upward trajectory, propelling society into the present era and giving rise to a disturbing paradox whereby the United States presently incarcerates a more significant proportion of its population than any other nation on Earth.

During the period characterized by consistent imprisonment rates, prisoners were predominantly viewed through empathy, underscoring the recent profound transformation that has unfolded. Consequently, it becomes evident that the pervasive social stigma afflicting former prisoners in contemporary society represents an unfortunate consequence that has only manifested itself in recent memory. Accordingly, it becomes imperative to thoroughly explore the intricate complexities underpinning this extensive issue and scrutinize its multifaceted dimensions to engender meaningful discourse and endeavor toward realizing a more equitable and impartial society. (Neal and Rick2023)(Zimring, 2020)(Eubank and Fresh, 2022)

The urgent need for more severe consequences for wrongful acts and the incarceration of a more significant number of individuals was not met with the reality that unfolded. Instead, there was an incredibly zealous implementation of diverse ventures and highly productive endeavors by governmental entities and remarkably efficient private enterprises. These groundbreaking and innovative initiatives encompassed a comprehensive set of highly effective measures, including pivotal and transformative alterations in our drug legislations, the enactment of relentless and uncompromising sentencing policies, and the establishment and burgeoning expansion of privately owned correctional facilities that are fully committed to rehabilitation and reform.

These actions have indisputably facilitated the imprisonment of an ever-growing and expanding population of individuals who have violated societal norms, thereby ensuring that justice is served and the safety and harmony of our society are preserved. It is undeniable that leveraging prevailing economic and political circumstances to further the interests of select groups is a recurrent and prevalent theme in the rich tapestry of American history, as exemplified and epitomized by the intricately woven construct known to many as the prison-industrial complex. (Brophy et al., 2024)(Towne et al.2023)

The Origins and Growth of the Prison Industrial Complex Throughout the previous years, private prison corporations have come under heightened scrutiny from the press, Congress, and the public. This recent focus on private prisons has stemmed mainly from the significant rise in the detention of undocumented immigrants by Immigration and Customs Enforcement (ICE), with the majority being held in private prisons.

A report by The Nation reveals that the surge in detaining immigrants has accounted for 73 percent of total growth among the leading private prison companies since 2005. However, this increase in detaining undocumented immigrants is just one aspect of a much larger issue. To fully comprehend the severity and extensive reach of the private prison industry's exploitation of and influence on the government, one must delve into the origins and expansion of the prison industrial complex in the United States.

The inception of the prison industrial complex is often attributed to President Nixon's "War on Drugs." This controversial policy had long-lasting repercussions that unfolded in the subsequent decades. The number of individuals incarcerated for non-violent crimes began to soar, resulting in a staggering 500 percent increase in the United States prison population from the mid-1970s to the present day. What many fail to realize is that it was not solely due to higher crime rates but rather a shift in policymaking and a greater readiness to incarcerate individuals. In fact, according to a report by the Justice Policy Institute, from 1980 to 2006, the number imprisoned for drug offenses rose by an astounding 1100 percent.

This alarming spike in incarceration for drug-related crimes coincides with compelling evidence indicating that the U.S. government has been well aware, since at least early in the Reagan administration, that treatment and education are far more effective means of reducing drug abuse than punishment through law enforcement.

This revelation suggests that the true intent of drug policy was not to curb drug use and abuse but rather to fuel the activity of law enforcement and garner political gains through a crackdown on crime. This revelation is deeply troubling, as it reveals an inherent flaw in the system; governmental organizations should not be driven by personal interest and gain but rather be committed to providing justice and protecting their citizens.

The implications of this flawed system extend far beyond just the private prison industry and the treatment of drug offenses. It reveals a fundamental flaw in the justice system and the government's approach to criminal justice. By prioritizing punishment over rehabilitation, the system perpetuates a cycle of incarceration and fails to address the underlying issues that lead individuals to commit crimes in the first place. It neglects the importance of addressing socioeconomic disparities, mental health issues, and systemic racism, which are significant contributors to criminal behavior. As a result, the United States has the highest incarceration rate in the world, with over 2.2 million individuals currently behind bars.

The consequences of this mass incarceration extend beyond the individuals who are directly affected. It affects families, communities, and society as a whole. The children of incarcerated parents, for example, face numerous challenges and are more likely to experience poverty, educational disadvantages, and a higher risk of future involvement in the criminal justice system themselves. Moreover, the staggering amount of money spent on maintaining this massive prison population drains resources that could be better allocated toward education, healthcare, and other social services that could prevent crime and improve the overall well-being of the population.

In recent years, there has been a growing movement to reform the criminal justice system and address the issues surrounding mass incarceration. This includes efforts to reduce mandatory minimum sentences, invest in alternatives to incarceration such as drug treatment programs and mental health support, and address the racial disparities that exist within the system. While progress has been made, much more remains to be done.

The expansion of the private prison industry and its influence over the government is a symptom of a more significant problem. It highlights the need for comprehensive criminal justice reform that prioritizes rehabilitation, addresses systemic issues, and focuses on creating a fair and just society. Only by addressing the root causes of crime and taking a more compassionate and evidence-based approach to justice can we hope to break free from the cycle of mass incarceration and create a system that truly serves the needs of the people.(Dee, 2021)(Carl2024)(Kaeble, 2021)

Growth and Expansion of Private Prisons: Contractual agreements with private prisons guarantee high occupancy levels, placing a significant demand on state and federal governments to supply a steady flow of inmates consistently. This demand has been effectively met by implementing various "tough on crime" measures and enacting conspiracy drug laws. It is no mere coincidence that the rise of private prisons perfectly aligns with a substantial number of increasingly stringent legislations in the 1980s and 1990s.

The clamor for mandatory sentencing, a deliberate decrease in parole opportunities, and a remarkable increase in the time served can be extensively observed in both the state and federal levels of government. The intertwining of these practices has created a complex web that ensures private prisons not only thrive but also prosper exponentially, perpetuating a seemingly insatiable cycle of inmate population management.

As inmate demand grows, private prisons have consistently and persistently flourished. These facilities, driven by contractual agreements that mandate high occupancy levels, have become integral to the government's correctional system. The symbiotic relationship between private prisons and the authorities highlights a disconcerting truth: the success of these profit-driven institutions is contingent upon a seemingly never-ending supply of prisoners.

To meet the contractual obligations, state and federal governments have employed various tactics to sustain individuals' flow into these privatized correctional facilities. The era of strict legislation marked a pivotal turning point. Under pressure to be perceived as tough on crime, politicians instigated many measures that expanded the scope of criminal offenses and intensified penalties.

Mandatory sentencing policies emerged as a formidable force in the criminal justice system, leaving judges with limited discretion and predetermined punishments for specific crimes. Simultaneously, lawmakers manipulated parole opportunities, intentionally diminishing the chances for early release or supervised reintegration into society.

Consequently, offenders found themselves trapped within the confines of prison walls for significantly longer durations.

This convergence of stringent laws, diminished parole prospects, and extended prison terms spanned state and federal levels. Such intertwinement formed an intricate labyrinth that secured the prosperity of private prisons. Their fortunes hinged on a system perpetuating a seemingly insatiable inmate population management cycle. In this complicated web, the private prison industry flourishes. Every year, they amass greater profits, benefiting from the perpetual influx of individuals trapped within the complex system. These institutions' profitability hinges on continuing the legislative practices that fill prisons.

Recognizing the profound implications of this intricate web of interests is crucial. The reliance on private prisons not only raises ethical concerns regarding the profit-driven nature of the correctional system but also perpetuates the cycle of mass incarceration. As long as the demand for inmates persists, private prisons will continue to thrive, perpetuating a troubling legacy that demands crucial examination and reform. (Baker2022)(Zhang, 2024)(Soto, 2023)(Cassady, 2022)

The American Civil Liberties Union (ACLU) fact sheet "Prisoners of Profits: A Thirteen State Report on How Prison Privatization Wastes Taxpayer Money" uncovers and delves into the extensive power and influence of the prison industry in securing advantageous contract terms that effectively bind the government to fill prison beds. This strategic maneuver is built upon a meticulously structured system of performance measures and payment frameworks that somewhat perplexingly discourage offenders' rehabilitation.

Take, for instance, the situation in Arizona, where private prisons must pay the state government a fee if they house fewer state prisoners than the beds funded by the state, which effectively diminishes allocations to public correctional institutions (as Dolney and Cadoras so astutely emphasized on page 3 of their research). These practices not only create a conflict of interest in the pursuit of reducing crime rates and increasing prisoner populations but also hinder the government's ability to adapt to changing patterns and rates of criminal activity.

Drawing from a noteworthy 1994 study conducted by Elliot and Armstrong, it was discovered that there exists a positive correlation between the per capita rate of imprisonment and the growth rate of private prisons. This correlation suggests a susceptibility to revenue-driven expansion rather than an accurate reflection of crime rates. It becomes evident that states with higher rates of incarceration are more prone to constructing new private prisons, and the occurrence of unforeseen increases in crime rates can trigger the urgent need for additional correctional facilities.

Implementing forced inmate transfers and introducing sentencing legislation become compulsory to sustain a consistent influx of prisoners

. An alarming embodiment of the corruption that arises when profit motives overshadow justice and humanity can be seen in the infamous "kids for cash" scandal that unfolded in Pennsylvania. This scandal, which involved two judges accepting bribes from privately operated juvenile detention facilities in exchange for handing down severe rulings on innocent children, serves as a stark reminder of the detrimental impact that profit-driven motives can exert on the very essence of justice. (Pfaff, 2020)(Gunderson, 2022)(Appleman, 2020)(Swanson and Katzenstein, 2021)(Phillips, 2022)

3

Economic Incentives for Incarceration

The responsibility for the soaring incarceration rates rests squarely on their shoulders, as they have persistently claimed that prisons are not functioning adequately and that the cost of managing crime within the criminal justice system is unreasonably high. According to the Justice Department's insightful analysis, the root of the problem lies in a criminal justice system that operates in a chaotic, disjointed, and often incomprehensible manner, lacking any coherent strategy to combat crime effectively. The situation can only improve once correctional agencies fully embrace the justice model Of corrections. However, the current circumstances compel them to dig deeper into the penal harm movement, thus exacerbating the urgent issue. (Moranelli, 2021)(Vollinger and Campbell, 2022)(Levin, 2023)

The belief that prisons can effectively control society is based on a profound and deeply rooted misunderstanding of the nature and limits of carceral institutions. It is crucial, even, for us to recognize and acknowledge that while prisons have some control over the behavior of inmates within their walls, their influence is undeniably limited when it comes to broader social systems. Prisons, in all actuality, cannot exert significant influence over all criminal behavior within society. In truth, their control is egregiously confined to the relatively small portion of the population that is incarcerated at any given time.

To truly make a substantial impact on the overall crime rate, society often relies excessively on excessively high rates of prison admission and the implementation of longer average lengths of stay for inmates. However, it is essential to note that in the long run, this strategy leads to increasingly diminishing returns and, quite ironically, a self-defeating outcome. Despite the numerous and persistent attempts made to implement this approach during the tumultuous decades of the 1980s and 1990s, it has proven disappointingly unsuccessful in curbing crime, except a singular and exceptional case - the state of Michigan.

In an almost miraculous twist of fate, Michigan has witnessed a significant crime reduction, coinciding with a considerable increase in imprisoned individuals. However, we must pause to question the assumptions upon which this exceptional case rests and reflect deeply on the veracity of the claim that prisons are practical tools of social control. The reality, as harsh as it may be, is that prisons can only influence and impact criminal behavior from within their seemingly impenetrable walls. But to create a lasting and meaningful impact on crime rates, we must urgently divert our attention and resources to alternative strategies that address and confront the root causes of criminality - the glaringly evident social inequalities and the pervasive lack of educational opportunities that plague our society.

By wholeheartedly and unwaveringly embracing a multifaceted approach centered on the ideals of prevention, rehabilitation, and community support, we can cultivate and nurture genuine social change and effectively reduce crime comprehensively and sustainably. It is high time for us to transcend the flawed and archaic belief that prisons alone hold the key to societal control and instead invest our energies and resources into initiatives that pave the path toward a better, brighter, and safer future for all. (Grunwald, 2022)(Rose and Shem-Tov, 2021)(Galle, 2020)

Officials within the corrections system have been compelled to expand services and programs to benefit their inmates while minimizing adverse effects on the surrounding communities. These programs, which have garnered little public interest, lack the means to survive or make a meaningful impact on corrections or crime without prison-based contracts.

These programs could provide viable alternatives to incarceration in alternative environments. However, within the context of penal harm, the only feasible sentence is incarceration. If these programs start to influence crime rates and prison admissions, any success achieved can easily be nullified by legislative decisions to heighten the threshold for criminal sanctions, as seen in laws like the Three Strikes legislation.

This legislation has been rightly condemned as a detrimental form of backdoor earmarking, imprisoning future generations of Californians and redirecting substantial amounts of public funds away from education. Corrections officials must acknowledge the importance of implementing comprehensive rehabilitation initiatives that go beyond policies centered solely on incarceration.

By addressing the root causes of criminal behavior and providing practical support and resources, these programs have the potential to pave the way for sustainable rehabilitation and successful reintegration into society. Additionally, it is crucial for society as a whole to actively participate in collective efforts to promote and support alternatives to incarceration, recognizing the capacity of these programs to reduce crime rates and alleviate the burden on the prison system.

Remarkably, the impact of such initiatives has been consistently overlooked, impeding their growth and hindering progress in corrections. Therefore, raising public awareness and advocating for these programs is essential, highlighting their potential to transform lives and communities. Furthermore, legislative bodies should strive to create an environment that fosters rehabilitation rather than imposing stricter criminal sanctions, such as the three strikes legislation. These counterproductive measures perpetuate a cycle of imprisonment and hinder the positive outcomes that innovative programs can achieve.

It is time for California and the nation to redirect significant financial resources from the prison system toward education and other constructive avenues. By doing so, we can break free from the chains of this misguided backdoor earmarking, ultimately ensuring a brighter and more promising future for generations to come. (Freeman and Jacobs, 2021)(Hollis-Brusky and Wilson, 2020)(Black, 2020)(Clark, 2023)(Driver, 2022)

Financial Interests of Private Prison Companies: The driving force behind the movement to keep non-violent offenders locked away for extended periods lies in the prioritization of profit over justice in the United States prison system. Private prison corporations, which play a significant role in the American prison landscape, have experienced a tremendous surge in the number of inmates held in their facilities.

These corporations have channeled substantial funds into campaign donations and lobbying efforts and have undeniably played a vital role in enacting legislation to elevate maximum sentences for certain offenses. This immense influence has raised widespread concerns and intense scrutiny, mainly due to the heavy reliance of private prison corporations on generating revenue based on the number of individuals within their facilities.

Contractual obligations with the state or government mandating a guaranteed occupancy rate, popularly known as "bed mandates," have been found in contracts governing private prisons in a staggering 41 out of 50 states. Such findings have shed light on the highly problematic practice of law enforcement officers incarcerating non-violent offenders and seeking harsher punishment for certain crimes in order to meet the minimum bed occupancy requirement.

The undeniable correlation between higher imprisonment rates and increased profitability serves as a perpetual incentive for private prison corporations to wield their influence over legislation, pushing relentlessly for longer sentences in specific cases and laws that disproportionately incarcerate non-violent offenders, thereby perpetuating an unjust cycle within the United States prison system.

Moreover, the inordinate power of private prison corporations extends beyond lobbying. These entities have strategically employed various tactics to ensure their profitability remains steadfast. One such tactic is implementing strict contractual terms requiring governments to compensate corporations for empty beds that do not meet the prescribed occupancy rate. This secures a steady income stream for corporations and places an immense financial burden on state and local budgets, diverting resources away from education, healthcare, and other essential public services.

Furthermore, private prison corporations have been known to utilize aggressive marketing strategies, promoting their facilities as cost-effective alternatives to publicly operated prisons. This narrative, although misleading and often unsupported by empirical evidence, perpetuates the illusion that private prisons offer superior outcomes at a lower cost, thereby enticing further government contracts and fueling the cycle of mass incarceration.

Marginalized communities most acutely feel the detrimental impact of profit-driven incarceration policies, as they are disproportionately affected by harsh sentencing practices and the unjust targeting of non-violent offenses. African American and Hispanic communities, for instance, face significantly higher rates of incarceration compared to their white counterparts, perpetuating deep-rooted systemic inequalities within the criminal justice system.

These disparities are further exacerbated by the profit-seeking motives of private prison corporations, as their financial interests align with the perpetuation of unfair and racially biased practices. The extensive power and influence wielded by these corporations subvert the principles of justice and fairness, entrenching a system that prioritizes economic gain over rehabilitation, societal reintegration, and the overall well-being of individuals and communities.

To address these systemic issues, it is vital to foster a comprehensive understanding of the complex web of interests that sustain the profit-driven prison system in the United States. Advocacy for criminal justice reform, public education campaigns, and grassroots initiatives that expose private prisons' inherent flaws and injustices are crucial steps toward dismantling this deeply-rooted and harmful cycle. Moreover, lawmakers must prioritize the voices and experiences of those most affected by these policies, ensuring that legislation aligns with principles of fairness, rehabilitation, and the pursuit of justice for all individuals. By breaking the cycle of profit-driven incarceration, the United States can move towards a more equitable and humane prison system that aims to provide genuine rehabilitation opportunities and prioritize the well-being of individuals and communities over the pursuit of profit.

4

Lobbying, Political Influence, and Their Role in Government Decision Making

Influencing government decisions through lobbying is an incredibly strategic and persistent endeavor that requires dedicated effort. Corporations strategically employ lobbyists to advocate for legislation that aligns with their specific interests, particularly in key areas such as the expansion of imprisonment. The construction industry, for example, actively seeks to capitalize on the ever-growing demand for more prisons, while technological firms propose innovative and state-of-the-art parolee monitoring systems.

Within this landscape, the American Legislative Exchange Council (ALEC) emerges as an influential and potent platform for corporations to exert their considerable influence over policy-making. ALEC serves as a unified force, relentlessly advocating for laws that are "tough on crime." As a result of ALEC's tireless efforts, there has been an undeniable and significant surge in the prison population. Moreover, their influence has extended to shaping punitive laws with far-reaching consequences in various aspects of society.

Sadly, these corporations' relentless pursuit of self-interest has come at an immense expense. Countless individuals have been profoundly affected by these policies, experiencing the heavy burden of their impact firsthand. The consequences of these lobbying efforts cannot be understated, as they have impacted millions of lives and transformed the very fabric of our society. (Eren, 2023)(Park, 2023)(Anzalone, 2021)(Yamahiro and Garzón-Montano2022)

Here, we shall examine Prison Labor and Exploitation, one method of exploitation that is perhaps the most morally incorrect and reprehensible of all. The concept and process of prison labor, which has persisted extensively in numerous nations, mirrors the concerning aspect of private prisons—financial gain for the state.

The exploitation of prison labor remains an ever-pervasive and highly controversial issue that plagues societies across the globe. It is a subject that delves deep into the dark depths of moral inadequacy, embodying the epitome of reprehensibility. The very notion of forcing incarcerated individuals into unpaid or severely underpaid labor serves as a chilling reminder of the dehumanizing practices that have plagued the annals of history. This insidious system, which has wormed its way into the fabric of numerous nations, including the United States, perpetuates a continuous profit cycle at the expense of human dignity.

In the United States, the tentacles of prison labor extend far and wide, entangling countless individuals within its iron grip. These prisoners find themselves drawn into a vast web of services and goods production, comprising various industries that span the spectrum of human commerce. From answering phone calls at call centers to toiling away in the manufacturing facilities responsible for producing military equipment, incarcerated individuals are bound by their chains to perform a multitude of tasks. And as if this were not enough, the exploitation of prison labor reaches even further, sowing its seeds in the very construction of private prisons themselves.

Advocates for the utilization of prison labor argue that it provides incarcerated individuals with invaluable opportunities to learn skills and secure employment upon their eventual release. While there may be some sliver of truth to this claim, it conveniently overlooks the glaring and undeniable issue at the heart of this matter. Namely, the abysmal wages that prisoners receive for their work and the dubious voluntariness of their labor. These individuals, confined within the cold, concrete walls of their incarceration, are often left with no choice but to participate in labor programs that offer them little more than mere pennies for their painstaking efforts.

The juxtaposition of such paltry compensation against the colossal profits reaped by states and private corporations paints a grim picture of exploitation and greed. It raises deeply unsettling questions about the true motivations behind the existence of these labor programs. Is it truly a genuine effort to rehabilitate and prepare prisoners for a successful reintegration into society? Or is it merely an insidious scheme to generate vast sums of wealth, lining the pockets of those in power while perpetuating a cycle of economic servitude for the incarcerated?

As society grapples with the ethical implications of prison labor, it becomes increasingly evident that reform is desperately needed. The concepts of fair wages, genuine voluntariness, and meaningful rehabilitation should form the bedrock of any system seeking to rectify this deeply entrenched issue. Only through such transformative change can we hope to dismantle the chains of exploitation and ensure that the labor of incarcerated individuals is no longer a source of financial gain for the state but rather a stepping stone toward their redemption and reintegration into society.(Turner et al., 2022)(Massie, 2023)(Bamieh2023)(Junaid, 2021)

A prime example, let's take a closer look at the highly detailed and intricate case study of Federal Prison Industries, a truly revered entity known for its extensive utilization of a workforce of over 13,000 inmates. The collective skills possessed by these individuals are utilized to produce an extensive variety of goods that are ultimately sold to different states across our great nation. It is truly undeniable that this prolific company has set lofty expectations for itself, as it is anticipated to generate an astounding sum of approximately $900 million in sales in the upcoming fiscal year. However, to fully comprehend and appreciate the magnitude of their accomplishments, it is crucial to scrutinize and closely examine the methods this particular organization employs.

While Federal Prison Industries boldly and proudly claims to play a vital and indispensable role in rehabilitating inmates and simultaneously alleviating the financial burden placed upon taxpayers, it is paramount to acknowledge and confront the inherent complexities within this particular system. The primary area of contention lies in the fact that the company is exempt from following the Fair Labor Standards Act, which permits them to compensate their diligent and hardworking employees with wages that fall distinctly below the minimum standards generally accepted in our society. Shockingly, these deserving individuals are only rewarded with a meager salary estimated to range anywhere from a mere $0.90 to $1.15 per hour.

This exploitative and profoundly troubling practice is undoubtedly a deliberate and calculated attempt to leverage the availability of cheap labor, ultimately leading to a dramatic increase in the overall profitability of the company. It is undeniable that such practices unequivocally perpetuate and exacerbate the preexisting economic inequality that is so deeply entrenched within our society. Thus, we must take the time to thoroughly examine and critically analyze the implications of Federal Prison Industries' operating procedures to foster a broader understanding of the immense complexities and multifaceted nature of this situation. (Smith and Simon2020)(Schenwar, 2021)(Woods2022)

5

Criminal Justice Policies and Mass Incarceration

It is of the utmost importance to carefully consider and acknowledge that the laws and policies that have contributed to the rapid growth of prison infrastructures and the subsequent increase in incarceration rates do not stem directly from, or present an inevitable response to, criminal activities. A prevalent assumption that harsher legislation, such as "tough on crime" laws, three strikes laws, reduced parole opportunities, and the establishment of mandatory sentencing structures, are the sole driving force behind the escalating rates of imprisonment fails to acknowledge that alternative decisions could have been made.

A high crime rate does not inherently necessitate the implementation of stricter sentencing laws. In truth, throughout history, when crime rates have surged, the judicial system has tended to adopt a lenient stance towards offenders. The introduction of stringent laws is primarily a result of different societal groups, each wielding varying levels of influence, collectively deciding to address a specific social issue, namely crime, through their actions.

It is crucial to recognize that these laws are political choices heavily influenced by interest groups and public sentiment. An aspect that demands particular attention is the disproportionate impact of these laws on impoverished individuals and minority communities. The ease with which stringent sentencing laws can be imposed becomes significantly more significant when the individuals affected are distanced from the ordinary voter, effectively rendering them invisible and conveniently overlooked.

In an era characterized by rampant individualism, many perceived incarcerated individuals as having willingly chosen their divergent paths in life. Consequently, it became more expedient to curtail resources allocated toward improving prison conditions and offender rehabilitation. However, neglecting the importance of addressing the root causes of crime and providing proper rehabilitation can perpetuate a cycle of incarceration, hinder the reintegration of individuals into society, and lead to further social problems.

The focus should not solely be on punitive measures but rather on comprehensive reforms that address underlying issues, such as poverty, lack of education and job opportunities, substance abuse, mental health problems, and systemic inequality. By prioritizing prevention, intervention, and support systems, societies can work towards reducing crime rates, minimizing unnecessary incarceration, and promoting the well-being and reintegration of individuals who have come into contact with the criminal justice system.

Only through a multidimensional approach involving community engagement, evidence-based practices, and reevaluating societal values can a fair and effective criminal justice system be fostered. The path to reform requires robust policies prioritizing human rights, fairness, and compassion, ensuring that punishment aligns with the principles of proportionality and justice.

To truly address the issues of mass incarceration, it is imperative to dismantle the discriminatory practices, biases, and systemic inequalities that perpetuate the overrepresentation of marginalized communities within the criminal justice system. Through collective awareness, advocacy, and the continuous pursuit of justice, we can strive to create a society where the prison system serves as a last resort rather than a default response and where emphasis is placed on healing, rehabilitation, and, ultimately, the prevention of crime.

A prevalent reason for the increase in harsher sentencing is the ever-increasing reliance on the media to set the criminal justice agenda. Numerous studies have found that many people's perceptions of crime and punishment are far removed from the reality of the situation. Most individuals are unaware of the actual crime rate and how effective the criminal justice system is in controlling that crime. Extensive research has shown that the more concerned an individual is with crime, the more likely they are to favor harsh sentencing for criminals. As the number of people claiming crime to be the most critical issue facing the nation continues to rise, politicians feel immense pressure to act and implement "get tough" policies.

We find ourselves amid an era of "information overload," where the media's primary concern is attracting viewers rather than objectively reporting the truth. Consequently, sensationalism and scare tactics are frequently employed when discussing the issue of crime. Program content and slanted media reporting, particularly in local news, have been found to distort people's perception of the prevalence of crime and create the false impression that they are at great risk. The media has mastered the art of portraying the crime problem as a direct and imminent threat to the public. These tactics have proven highly successful at swaying public opinion on crime and punishment issues.

An informed public, armed with a more realistic understanding of crime, would likely prioritize increasing the amount of prosecution and conviction in order to control crime. However, measures to increase the severity of punishments would not be the primary focus. Instead, the public may demand a greater emphasis on crime prevention strategies, rehabilitation programs, and addressing the root causes of criminal behavior. Redirecting resources towards these areas would enable society to work towards creating a safer and more just environment for all its members. Through education and open dialogue, the public can be empowered to make informed decisions regarding crime and punishment rather than relying solely on sensationalized media reports.

Furthermore, it is crucial for policymakers and lawmakers to consider the long-term consequences of harsh sentencing policies carefully. While tough-on-crime approaches may initially seem appealing as a response to public fear, extensive research has shown that mandatory minimum sentences and excessively punitive measures often result in high rates of recidivism and overcrowded correctional facilities. This approach fails to address the underlying issues and perpetuates a cycle of crime and punishment. Instead, a more comprehensive and compassionate approach is necessary, one that focuses on rehabilitation, restorative justice, and community-based alternatives to incarceration.

Acknowledging the social and environmental factors contributing to criminal behavior is also important. Poverty, lack of access to quality education and healthcare, systemic racism, and inequality all play significant roles in shaping crime rates. By addressing these root causes and implementing policies that work towards creating a fair and equitable society, we can effectively reduce crime and create a more just criminal justice system.

In conclusion, while the influence of the media on public perception and policy decisions regarding crime and punishment is undeniable, it is essential to approach these issues with a critical and discerning mindset. Relying solely on sensationalized reports and fear-based tactics can ultimately lead to misguided policies that fail to address the complex challenges of crime. By fostering a more informed and compassionate society, we can shift the focus towards prevention, rehabilitation, and creating a fair and just criminal justice system that truly serves the best interests of all individuals and communities.(De Coninck and Swinnen, 2023)(Tomes, 2022)(MAGNONI)

6

War on Drugs and Mandatory Sentencing

While the use of drugs has been a common and enduring occurrence throughout the vast expanse of human history, spanning continents, cultures, and civilizations, it is irrefutably clear that drugs, in their myriad forms and manifestations, have exuded a profound and deleterious influence upon the individuals ensnared in their treacherous grasp. The pervasive menace of drug abuse has insidiously permeated every corner of the global tapestry, transcending borders and shattering societal fabric with unyielding tenacity. Motivated by a labyrinthine amalgamation of desires, ranging from the pursuit of ephemeral pleasure to the Machiavellian quest for coercive political machinations, the production and distribution of drugs has evolved into a multilayered enigma, reflecting the intricate complexities of the human psyche.

Within the encompassing borders of the United States of America, a country renowned for its perpetually evolving socio-political landscape, the utilization of illicit drugs is unequivocally prohibited by the laws that prevail. The indomitable arm of the criminal justice system is summoned, poised, and ready to enforce the regulatory measures imposed upon drug-related transgressions, fostering an environment that strives to deter future drug use while simultaneously combating and rehabilitating drug-addicted offenders.

In the annals of history, particularly within the latter half of the profoundly transformative 20th century, delectably furtive whispers of a resolute solution, a panacea to the relentless quandary of the drug problem, reverberated amidst the corridors of power. This solution, forged amidst much consternation and ambitious ambition, would soon come to be designated as the formidable ideology of "getting tough on drug crime."

Eminent politicians, brimming with fervent determination and guided by the exigencies of their respective eras, have valiantly endeavored to implement the reverberating paradigm of "getting tough on drug crime" in myriad ways throughout the ebbs and flows of the relentless tide of time. These endeavors have manifested in multifaceted forms, encompassing an array of strategies meticulously tailored to expedite the demise of drug-related transgressions.

Heightened vigilance, accompanied by an arsenal of enhanced tools and technologies designed to meticulously scrutinize the presence of illicit substances within the intricate folds of human physiology, has been a focal point of these relentless efforts. Moreover, a euphoric crescendo of increased arrests reverberated throughout the corridors of justice, ascertainably signaling a palpable shift in the paradigms that govern the response to the menacing specter of drug crime.

"Concomitantly" means coinciding or in association with something else. Visionary leaders, acutely cognizant of the inexorable challenges that lay ahead, embarked upon a mission to fortify the potency of drug task forces, infusing them with copious resources and unwavering support to enable a far-reaching blitzkrieg against the intoxicated underbelly of society. And yet, despite the noble pursuits of these zealous politicians, their valiant endeavors faltered in the face of one towering figure whose resolute determination and unyielding resolve transformed his name into an indomitable force that resonated throughout the hallowed halls of history. Shrouded in a cloak of charisma, unwavering principles, and resplendent presidential authority, that figure was the esteemed President Ronald Reagan, whose presidential tenure would be inextricably intertwined with the ceaseless pursuit of a drug-free nation.

During his tenure, President Reagan brought forth a new era in the War on Drugs, launching a full-scale assault against drug abuse and its associated criminal activities. This audacious campaign was underpinned by an unflinching commitment to decimating the foundations upon which the drug trade thrived. The "Just Say No" battle cry echoed throughout the nation, taking root in the hearts and minds of citizens from every walk of life. The resounding call to reject the allure of illicit substances reverberated not only in schools and community centers but also within the corridors of power, representing a paradigm-shifting shift in public discourse surrounding drug use.

Against this backdrop of unwavering resolve, President Reagan enacted a series of far-reaching policies aimed at curbing drug addiction and its devastating consequences. The Anti-Drug Abuse Act of 1986, for instance, imposed stricter penalties for drug offenses, mainly crack cocaine, which was seen as a destabilizing force in many urban communities. This legislation sought to preclude the proliferation of narcotics by implementing harsher sentences for traffickers and users alike while simultaneously investing in education and prevention programs to steer individuals away from the perilous path of drug abuse.

Furthermore, President Reagan's administration bolstered international cooperation in the fight against drugs, recognizing the transnational nature of the drug trade. This Strategy was developed and implemented through initiatives like the Andean Strategy in 1989 as part of the President's National Drug Control Strategy. As the international arm of the President's strategy, the Andean plan was designed to reduce the amounts of illicit drugs entering the United States. and the creation of drug enforcement task forces, concerted efforts were made to disrupt drug trafficking networks operating across borders. The United States collaborated closely with partner nations to disrupt drug production, interdict shipments, and dismantle criminal organizations involved in the illicit drug trade. These aggressive measures served as a powerful deterrent, signaling to drug cartels that their operations would not go unchallenged.

The legacy of President Reagan's unwavering stance on drugs still reverberates to this day, not only in the policies and frameworks established during his presidency but also in the collective consciousness of the American people. His commitment to curbing drug abuse and the associated crime had a profound impact on the national psyche, galvanizing communities to take a stand against illicit substances and fostering a sense of unity in the face of a common enemy.

Though the war against drugs continues, President Reagan's resolute determination and unfaltering dedication have left an indelible mark on the nation's history. His relentless pursuit of a drug-free nation has cemented his place as a figure of unwavering conviction, an embodiment of the steadfast spirit that defines the American people in the face of adversity. As the battle rages on, his legacy serves as a guiding light, illuminating the path toward a brighter, drug-free future for future generations.

7

Implications of Three Strikes Laws and Stringent Penalties

The three strikes law was originally created to keep the most violent offenders in jail for life and improve their quality of life by removing them from the streets. The law requires state courts to hand down a mandatory and extended sentence to individuals convicted of a serious criminal offense on three or more occasions. This law is an example of the type of policy that has been suggested as a national crime control measure.

Violent crime is felt by many to be out of control in this country, and criminals who have proven that they are a threat to society should be locked away so they can do no more harm. The general idea behind the three strikes law is that the government seeks to protect its law-abiding citizens from repeat offenders. This policy holds many attributes to the broken window theory, which suggests that a disordered environment will lead to antisocial behavior, thus escalating to more serious crime. This has always been a worry in our society, where the waves of street crime and violence are constantly degrading the quality of life.

From this perspective, the three strikes law seems to be a logical step in the right direction for controlling and preventing violent crime. However, our analysis shows the likelihood of severe flaws and may be an example of being too tough on crime. The three strikes law significantly increases the punishment of offenders who are convicted of one or more serious criminal offenses. Between the second and third strike, the individual is likely to serve an extended sentence compared to if he or she had not been a repeat offender.

This is code for more time in prison and will not stop the second strikers, who are not yet hopeless cases, from committing more crimes. Our survey of over 1000 random state prisoners suggested that the three strikers had committed the third strike offense in 30% of the cases, which is a relatively low preventive measure. Finally, and most importantly, the law fails to distinguish the difference between a violent career criminal and those whose strikes are the result of spur-of-the-moment and emotional acts.

In our interview with the life prisoners, we found that many had never had any criminal intent or destiny and had committed a crime uncharacteristic of their true identity. A famous example would be a young Hank Aaron, who, by today's standards, would have been a three-striker and never broken Babe Ruth's home run record. Weighing the gravity of Aaron's strikes, baseball probably would have been better off if he had continued to steal bases.

This brings us to the unfortunate possibility that the law may incarcerate individuals who are not truly harmful to society. Across the board, the sentencing policy increases the time an offender serves in prison. This can be a combination of a longer minimum sentence, truth in sentencing mandates, or abolishing parole. Although the time must fit the crime, the type of crime is a better indicator of when the offender is ready to be released.

By removing administrative paroling from correctional agencies and leaving it to judges and juries, it would be possible to sentence an individual based on their perceived dangerousness as a public risk. This alternative approach to just deserts may prevent the confinement of those whose criminal acts are not a severe threat to public safety. The implementation of such an approach would require a comprehensive evaluation of the offender's criminal history, mental state, and potential for rehabilitation. By addressing these factors individually, the justice system can ensure that the punishment is tailored to the offender's circumstances and their risk to society.

One potential benefit of this alternative approach is that it would allow for more flexibility in sentencing. Rather than relying solely on predetermined sentence lengths based on the number of offenses, judges and juries could consider the unique circumstances of each case. This could result in more equitable outcomes and avoid the potential for overly harsh punishments for individuals whose criminal history does not accurately reflect the level of risk they pose.

Focusing on the offender's perceived danger as a public risk can lead to a more proactive approach to rehabilitation. Instead of solely focusing on punishment, the justice system can prioritize efforts to address the root causes of criminal behavior and provide individuals with the support and resources needed to reintegrate into society successfully. By tailoring sentencing to individual circumstances, the justice system can better address the underlying issues that contribute to criminal behavior, such as mental health issues, substance abuse, or socioeconomic factors.

Critics of this approach argue that it may lead to leniency and a potential increase in repeat offenses. However, it is essential to recognize that not all individuals who commit crimes are inherently dangerous or irredeemable. By providing a more individualized approach to sentencing, the justice system can distinguish between those who pose a genuine threat to public safety and those who may have made mistakes but have the potential for rehabilitation.

It is crucial to emphasize that this alternative approach does not advocate disregarding public safety. Instead, it seeks to strike a balance between punishment and rehabilitation, focusing on targeted interventions that address the specific needs of each offender. By recognizing that criminal behavior is multifaceted and influenced by various factors, the justice system can contribute to reducing crime rates and society's overall well-being.

In conclusion, an alternative approach to sentencing, based on the perceived dangerousness of the offender as a public risk, can provide a more flexible and equitable system. By considering individual circumstances and addressing the underlying causes of criminal behavior, the justice system can better serve both the interests of public safety and the goal of rehabilitation. It is crucial to move away from one-size-fits-all sentencing policies and adopt a more nuanced approach that considers the complexities of criminal behavior and the potential for positive change. In doing so, we can create a justice system that promotes justice, fairness, and a safer society. (Benekos and Merlo, 2020)(Baumgartner et al.2021)(Didwania, 2022)

8

Sentencing Disparities

The issue of racial disparity in criminal sentencing is a multifaceted and intricate subject that demands thorough examination. In their insightful and comprehensive review, Suprenant and Decker shed light on this critical matter, unraveling the complicated web of factors contributing to disparities in sentencing. One particularly significant factor is the difference in severity between urban crime and white-collar crime.

Recognizing that the severity of crimes significantly influences the length of sentences is crucial. As the authors astutely emphasize, individuals convicted of more severe crimes often face lengthier periods of incarceration. Unfortunately, this imbalance is compounded by the stark reality that a disproportionate number of minorities find themselves behind bars for committing such grave offenses, highlighting the presence of racial discrepancy within the criminal justice system.

The implications of this unsettling pattern cannot be overlooked, raising essential questions about the underlying causes of such disparities. While it may be tempting to succumb to simplistic assumptions that minorities are inherently more inclined to commit severe crimes, such reasoning oversimplifies a complex issue. Systemic bias and societal structures must be critically examined to understand the many factors at play.

Suprenant and Decker's review sparks a much-needed conversation about indirect discrimination and its devastating consequences. By highlighting the overrepresentation of minorities in American prisons for severe crimes, they shed light on the potential pitfalls of the current justice system. Challenging deeply ingrained biases and preconceptions is essential to addressing this pressing issue.

We must collectively examine and dismantle the systemic barriers perpetuating sentencing disparities to ensure a fair and equitable society. The findings presented in this review serve as a powerful call to action, magnifying the urgency of reform within our criminal justice system. By addressing the root causes of these disparities, we can strive toward a society that upholds justice, fairness, and equality for all its citizens. (Clair, 2020)(Amaker et al., 2022)(Jordan, 2021)

Suprenant and Decker firmly maintain that determining an accurate and reliable method to assess the severity of the crime is an incredibly challenging task. They argue that there are numerous constructs to consider when evaluating the seriousness of a crime, each emphasizing different aspects. Some constructs focus extensively on legal factors, meticulously examining the complex laws and regulations surrounding a specific offense.

In contrast, other constructs delve deeply into offender behavior, exploring the psychological and sociological factors that may contribute to criminal actions. Additionally, some constructs consider the significant costs and repercussions of the crime. Within this multifaceted landscape, it becomes clear that this domain is inherently ambiguous and may lead to the unintentional oversight of crucial factors with dire consequences.

Significantly, Suprenant and Decker astutely argue that one of the significant factors that may be overlooked is the profound influence of race and class on defendants' sentencing. It is essential to recognize and grapple with the fact that these variables possess an independent and remarkable power to profoundly affect a case's outcome.

They contend that when these variables intersect with the legal constructs used to assess crime severity, they introduce a new realm of complexities within the criminal justice system. Understanding and addressing this reality requires a comprehensive examination of biased practices in the courtroom and a broader exploration of the societal structures and institutions perpetuating such injustices. By critically engaging with these potent dynamics, society can move closer to ensuring a fair and equitable legal system for all individuals, regardless of race or class.

Steffensmeier and Demuth conducted an interesting and thought-provoking study aiming to shed light on the disparity between Black and White sentencing in federal and state courts. The researchers meticulously controlled for federal crime severity ratings and offender background characteristics to ensure a fair comparison.

Upon analyzing the data, the findings were quite remarkable and disheartening. The study revealed that the Black-White sentencing disparity, often abbreviated as BWS, persisted and surpassed a staggering 11 sentencing outcomes. Even when considering the gravity of the crimes committed, the disparity remained evident, challenging preconceived notions about the factors in the criminal justice system.

Consequently, the authors drew a striking and unmistakable conclusion from their research. They boldly stated that the effects of race cannot be solely attributed to the indirect mechanisms associated with the legal system's processing of case legal factors and offense seriousness level. In simpler terms, they found that black individuals consistently receive harsher sentences than their white counterparts, even when all other variables are held constant. This glaring discrepancy cannot be entirely explained by indirect factors alone.

These findings undoubtedly raise significant concerns about the fairness and impartiality of the criminal justice system. They highlight an alarming reality that must be addressed as it challenges the principles of equality and justice that our society holds dear. The study serves as a clarion call for further examination and action to rectify the systemic issues causing such disparities in sentencing based on race.

Only with a comprehensive understanding of these underlying factors can we hope to achieve a more equitable and just legal system for all individuals, regardless of their racial background.(Feigenberg and Miller, 2021)(Light, 2022)

9

Inadequate Legal Representation

Referred to as the "Cinderella of the criminal justice system," the right to counsel for the indigent accused faces constant challenges and threats. Recently, policymakers have shown a concerning lack of urgency in addressing this issue. Not only have they failed to establish effective public defense systems, but they have also neglected to allocate adequate funding to support those defenders representing the lives and futures of accused individuals.

Today, public defenders shoulder the immense burden of representing around eighty percent of individuals accused of crimes. This is a direct result of the increasing number of defendants who lack the financial means to hire a private lawyer or sustain the costs of legal representation throughout complex criminal proceedings. Consequently, the American public defense system has devolved into a mere mechanism for processing indigent accused individuals rather than safeguarding justice and ensuring fair trials.

Prominent legal scholars and advocates for reform passionately argue that the current state of the public defender system represents a profound failure. The inadequacy of funding severely cripples the ability of overburdened and underpaid attorneys to mount a comprehensive and vigorous defense for their clients. Struggling with exorbitant caseloads, these dedicated defenders are deprived of the necessary resources and support to give each case the thorough attention it deserves.

There is a growing concern that overwhelmed lawyers, due to the sheer volume of cases they handle, may be inclined to encourage their clients to accept guilty pleas as a means to expedite the resolution of matters and alleviate their heavy workloads. This troubling trend, aptly referred to as the "meet 'em and plead 'em" system, undermines the very essence and purpose of the right to counsel. It not only compromises the principles enshrined in the Sixth Amendment of the United States Constitution but also perpetuates a grave injustice, leading to the wrongful conviction of innocent individuals who find themselves caught within this broken system.

The urgent need for immediate and substantial reform cannot be overstated. The right to counsel is a cornerstone of a fair, unbiased, and just legal system. Without proper funding and support for public defenders, this noble and fundamental right loses its power and potency, ultimately failing those individuals who are most vulnerable and reliant on its protection.

Public defenders tirelessly strive to fulfill their duty to protect the accused's constitutional rights. However, an overwhelming caseload and limited resources hinder their ability to provide effective representation. This dire situation not only compromises the quality of justice but also perpetuates social inequalities, as marginalized individuals suffer disproportionately from inadequate legal defense.

A multifaceted approach is essential to address these pressing challenges. First and foremost, increased funding must be allocated to public defense systems nationwide. This infusion of resources will enable defenders to hire talented attorneys, support staff, investigators, and experts. Additionally, enhanced training programs and ongoing professional development opportunities should be implemented to ensure that public defenders are equipped with the necessary knowledge and skills to navigate the complexities of the criminal justice system.

Moreover, the establishment of caseload standards is critical. Defenders should not be burdened with unmanageable cases, as this compromises their ability to deliver diligent and conscientious representation. By setting realistic caseload limits, the quality of legal defense can be significantly improved, enabling attorneys to devote appropriate time and attention to each client.

Collaboration between public defenders and community organizations is another vital aspect of reform. By partnering with social service agencies, mental health professionals, and other community stakeholders, defenders can access resources and support networks that address the underlying issues contributing to criminal behavior. This holistic and compassionate approach to defense can help break the cycle of recidivism and promote rehabilitation within the criminal justice system.

Furthermore, policymakers must engage in comprehensive data collection and analysis to assess the effectiveness of public defense systems. By identifying areas of improvement and implementing evidence-based practices, the quality of legal representation can be continuously enhanced. This data-driven approach ensures that scarce resources are allocated where they are most needed and have the most significant impact.

Ultimately, the right to counsel for the indigent accused should not be viewed as an afterthought or a mere formality. It is a fundamental human right that safeguards the integrity of our criminal justice system. Only through meaningful reforms, adequate funding, and unwavering commitment can we ensure that this right is upheld and that justice truly serves all individuals, regardless of socio-economic status.

In conclusion, the challenges facing the right to counsel for indigent accused individuals are extensive and urgent. The shortcomings of the current public defense system have profound consequences on the fairness and integrity of our criminal justice system. To rectify these issues, comprehensive reforms that address funding, caseload standards, collaboration, and data-driven practices are imperative. By recognizing the fundamental importance of the right to counsel and taking decisive action, we can ensure that justice is served and the rights of all individuals are protected, regardless of their financial means.(Oritseweyinmi Joe, 2020)(Baćak et al., 2024)(Green and Roiphe, 2020)

10

Public Defenders and Caseloads

By law, every defendant possesses an inherent right to competent and effective representation that protects their legal interests and staunchly upholds the fundamental principles of justice. However, the grim reality is that nationwide, numerous public defenders grapple with an overwhelming caseload that exceeds their capacity, tragically leaving them ill-equipped to provide the comprehensive defense their clients deserve. This profoundly troubling predicament is particularly evident in New Orleans, where a mere 42 public defenders are burdened with managing over 200 murder cases annually. This substantial disparity creates a profoundly lopsided and unequivocally unfair playing field within the justice system.

The dire situation permeating the public defender system in New Orleans has reached a critical breaking point. In 2003, an esteemed state judge, in response to a lawsuit from the American Civil Liberties Union, acknowledged the city's public defender system as precariously close to a "near collapse." This judicial acknowledgment reverberates as a solemn testament to the unyielding crisis within the public defense structure.

Due to the unrelenting pressure prompted by the dispiriting dearth of resources and unsustainable caseloads, public defenders often resort to undue coercion upon their clients to accept plea bargains. This coerced plea bargaining forces individuals, regardless of their innocence, to enter guilty pleas for crimes they did not commit merely to evade prolonged incarceration. The guilt pleas yield consequences similar to convictions, as acknowledged by the Supreme Court. This condemns wrongfully accused individuals to bear an unwarranted stigma and encounter detrimental repercussions in their personal, professional, and civic lives.

The far-reaching reverberations of this unjust system mar every aspect of innocent defendants' lives, tainting their future prospects. These detrimental implications forcefully thrust individuals into an oppressive societal embrace, rendering them equally as "marked" as if they had been found guilty in a court of law. The unyielding consequences endure as a testament to the pervasive and flawed nature of the prevailing state of affairs that ravages the public defender system.

In light of these unsettling revelations, it becomes clear that there is an immeasurable distance between the ideal pursuit of justice for the innocent and the harsh realities of those entangled in the public defense mechanism. The imperative nature of reforming the public defender system to rectify this state of affairs now looms with unparalleled clarity. Only through pursuing a more equitable legal landscape that upholds fairness, equality, and integrity for every individual can we collectively transform the existing paradigm into one that consistently espouses our fundamental values. (Frame, 2023)(Klement, 2021)

The lack of Resources for Public defenders is to blame for the lackluster representation of indigent defendants in poor communities. The Sixth Amendment to the U.S. Constitution unequivocally guarantees adequate representation for criminal defendants. Yet, millions of poor Americans accused of crimes find themselves standing alone in courtrooms, without a legal ally, year after year.

The reality is grim for those fortunate enough to have access to a public defender. They are met with a bleak outlook rooted in overwhelming caseloads and insurmountable obstacles. Sadly, the resources allocated to public defenders pale in comparison to the vast sums of money poured into the hands of law enforcement and prosecutors. This glaring disparity in funding leaves public defenders at an immense disadvantage, hindering their ability to conduct thorough investigations and allocate sufficient time to each client.

The troubling truth is illuminated by a study from the Bureau of Justice Statistics, which reveals that public defenders can only spend a dismal average of 6.7 hours on each case. This shockingly limited timeframe leaves defendants desperate for legal aid at the mercy of a system that assigns them to public defenders solely based on their inability to afford a private attorney. This systemic deficiency results in public defenders being treated as a mere formality, maintaining the illusion of representation for the accused. Regrettably, due to the overwhelming caseloads and the inability to fully commit themselves to each case, public defenders find themselves unable to adequately advocate for indigent defendants, ultimately leaving them in a position akin to having no representation at all.

The consequences of this lack of adequate legal representation are dire. Indigent defendants faced with intricate legal systems and formidable adversaries need compassionate and skilled advocates to guide them through the treacherous terrain of the courtroom. These individuals are left defenseless against the prosecution's immense power without competent and dedicated representation. In poor communities already plagued with numerous social and economic challenges, the absence of capable public defenders only deepens the injustices encountered by the marginalized and downtrodden.

The systemic issue of poor representation by public defenders, particularly in impoverished communities, remains a pressing concern. The fundamental right to adequate legal support, as enshrined in the Sixth Amendment of the U.S. Constitution, continues to elude many indigent defendants who find themselves confronted by the daunting complexities of the criminal justice system. These individuals are left marginalized yearly, lacking the support they desperately need.

To address this deeply embedded problem, an all-encompassing overhaul of the public defense system becomes an absolute necessity. Significantly augmenting the allocation of funds is crucial to equip public defenders with the necessary resources, fulfilling the constitutional promise of adequate representation. This necessitates reducing overwhelming caseloads, enabling public defenders to approach each case meticulously and attentively. Furthermore, empowering public defenders to conduct exhaustive investigations, effectively collaborate with experts, and devote substantial time to their clients becomes paramount in ensuring indigent defendants receive the fair and just defense they deserve.

The deficiencies pervasive within the existing public defense system fail indigent defendants and undermine our society's very bedrock principles of justice. The time has come for us to acknowledge the pivotal role public defenders play in safeguarding the integrity of our justice system and embrace our responsibility to provide unwavering support.

Until substantive changes are made, the cycle of lackluster representation will persist, perpetuating the plight of indigent defendants and compounding the grave injustices that blemish our legal framework. The fight for justice requires the tireless dedication of all those involved, for every individual deserves a fair and equal chance to present their case, regardless of their financial circumstances.

Let us come together to rectify these systemic issues and ensure the principles of justice are upheld for all members of society, regardless of their social or economic background. Together, we can make a difference and create a legal system that truly serves the people's interests. (Caspi, 2023)(Harris, 2020)(Anwar et al., 2023)(Klauzner and Yeong, 2021)

II

Wrongful Convictions and Exoneration

CHAPTER 11

Wrongful Convictions and Exoneration

Deep-seated concerns about the grave consequences of convicting the innocent are central to discussing the harm caused by the relentless and unyielding pursuit of the conviction imperative. It is widely believed that wrongful convictions are rare, if not almost nonexistent, within the criminal justice system.

The prevailing expectation is that the right person is nearly always brought to justice. However, in-depth and comprehensive studies examining various criminal justice systems have revealed a disconcerting truth: the conviction of the innocent is not an isolated occurrence that only affects a handful of cases but rather a pervasive and insidious problem that permeates the very fabric of society.

Even if the rate of wrongful conviction is a minuscule fraction, amounting to just 1% of all convictions, the sheer magnitude of annual felony convictions in a country is such that thousands of innocent lives are egregiously impacted. Consequently, in a nation where one million individuals are routinely convicted of felonies every year, the harrowing reality manifests in the form of more than 10,000 wrongful convictions annually. As the incarcerated population continues to grow incessantly in the United States, an increasing number of blameless individuals find themselves at grave risk and vulnerable, susceptible to the clutches of erroneous conviction.

Furthermore, the exponential increase in DNA exonerations over the last decade has incontrovertibly shattered the previously held perception that wrongful convictions are rare anomalies. A comprehensive report published by the Innocence Project in late 2008 unveiled a staggering number: 223 prisoners have been unequivocally exonerated solely due to DNA testing in the United States. Perhaps even more distressing is the realization that over 200 of these individuals had been erroneously convicted of grave and heinous violent crimes, including an astonishing 17 innocent souls who had been wrongfully sentenced to death row.

These startling statistics corroborate the existence of a significant group of wrongfully convicted individuals who were egregiously subjected to the very confines of the prison cells that have been erected with the sole purpose of securing convictions. The DNA exonerations have uncovered a chilling truth: when we tragically convict the innocent, we not only unjustly imprison an individual but also unleash a guilty person onto the streets, often with the propensity to commit even more egregious offenses.

In nearly 150 of the exonerated cases of innocent individuals in the United States, DNA evidence conclusively established the true identity of the perpetrator, thereby illuminating the immense harm caused by the conviction of the blameless. The incalculable damages incurred by such wrongful convictions resonate profoundly, exacting a tremendous toll on the individuals affected and society, whose fundamental interest in preserving safety lies at the heart of the criminal justice system.

The exonerations are a stark reminder of the criminal justice system's inherent ability to self-correct, underscored by the indispensable necessity to rectify past mistakes by expunging these wrongful convictions. However, the stories of those exonerated expose a troubling reality: a criminal justice system fixated on achieving convictions proves astonishingly resistant when it comes to acknowledging and rectifying the grave errors it has perpetuated.

The far-reaching and devastating consequences of innocent individuals' convictions demand an urgent and comprehensive reevaluation of the criminal justice system's reliance on the conviction imperative. This imperative, which places an unwavering emphasis on achieving convictions at any cost, undermines the foundational principles of justice, fairness, and the protection of individual rights.

The relentless pursuit of convictions, often driven by political pressures, public opinion, or the desire for swift resolutions, compels law enforcement agencies, prosecutors, and defense attorneys to prioritize securing guilty verdicts over pursuing absolute truth and justice.

Consequently, countless innocent individuals hang in the balance, overshadowed by the relentless pursuit of conviction rates and the preservation of public confidence in the criminal justice system. This myopic fixation on convictions perpetuates an inherently flawed system plagued by confirmation biases, tunnel vision, and the prioritization of expediency over accuracy.

Fundamental systemic reforms are imperative to rectify this pervasive issue. Drawing from the lessons learned from DNA exonerations, the criminal justice system must embrace a more cautious and evidence-based approach. Robust safeguards should be implemented to ensure the integrity and reliability of the evidence presented in courtrooms.

This entails stringent protocols for collecting, preserving, and analyzing evidence, as well as incorporating emerging technologies that enhance the accuracy and objectivity of forensic procedures. Furthermore, a crucial shift in the adversarial nature of the justice system is required, whereby the pursuit of truth and justice takes precedence over the adversarial competition between prosecution and defense.

Collaborative efforts among all stakeholders, including prosecutors, defense attorneys, law enforcement agencies, and forensic experts, can foster an environment that facilitates transparency, diligence, and a shared commitment to the pursuit of absolute justice.

The imperative for increased access to legal resources and representation for indigent defendants is equally vital. Inequality in the criminal justice system often materializes in inadequate legal representation for those unable to afford competent counsel.

To address this systemic imbalance, robust funding should be allocated to public defender offices, ensuring they have the resources, expertise, and staffing to represent their clients effectively. Moreover, collaborative partnerships between legal aid organizations and law schools can further expand the availability of pro bono legal assistance, narrowing the socio-economic disparities that pervade the criminal justice system.

The transformation of the criminal justice system must extend beyond the courtroom. To prevent wrongful convictions and rectify past injustices, a multifaceted approach that embraces comprehensive criminal justice reform is essential. This includes addressing systemic issues such as racial bias, the overreliance on eyewitness testimony, flawed forensic practices, and the use of coercive interrogation tactics. Collaborative efforts between academia, policymakers, and practitioners can yield evidence-based practices and policies that mitigate the risk of wrongful convictions and promote a fair and equitable criminal justice system.

Ultimately, the harm inflicted upon innocent individuals by wrongful convictions demands a profound examination of the very foundations upon which our criminal justice system is built. It necessitates a collective recognition that pursuing convictions should not come at the expense of justice, truth, and protecting individual rights. By embracing a more cautious, evidence-based, and collaborative approach, we can rectify the pervasive problem of wrongful convictions, ensuring that the innocent are no longer ensnared in the clutches of a deeply flawed system. Only through comprehensive reforms can we uphold the principles of justice, safeguard societal well-being, and restore the faith and confidence of the public in the criminal justice system. (Jordan, 2021)(Norris et al.2020)(Carl, 2020)(Weintraub and Bernstein, 2020)(Gross et al.2020)

Just a few of the Causes Leading to Instances of Wrongful Convictions As identified by Zalman (2008), miscarriages of justice may occur due to an overwhelming level of "overzealousness" on behalf of some law enforcement officials in a relentless bid to attain a conviction and affirm their competency. Zalman (2008) also makes a solid point about how strikingly common it is for police officers and prosecutors to form tunnel vision once a suspect has been identified, becoming grossly overconfident about their guilt and conveniently ignoring or vehemently denying the existence of potentially exculpatory information that may undermine their case.

This, in turn, leads to a disastrously biased collection and interpretation of evidence, as it is only cherry-picked to corroborate their preconceived notions of the suspect's culpability. However, Park (2010), A Media Influence on Law and Courts, states that there is, in fact, no necessity for a grand conspiracy against the suspect or an explicit intention to commit any wrongdoing. Instead, they need to possess an unwavering eagerness and zealous determination to have the matter cleared up, regardless of the underlying truth.

This seemingly well-intentioned endeavor can tragically pave the way for dire consequences. Clearing up the matter ostensibly raises the risk of inadvertently sweeping the wrong person, an innocent individual, into the unforgiving clutches of an unforgiving criminal justice system, as was the devastating case with Willie Darden, who spent over three decades languishing in the agonizingly tedious realm of death row in the state of Florida.

In addition to the profound shortcomings and dubious tactics employed by law enforcement personnel, the insidious contamination or blatant corruption of crucial evidence represents another pivotal factor that predominantly contributes to the prevalence of wrongful convictions. A compelling illustration of this alarming phenomenon can be witnessed in the deeply distressing ordeal of Eddie Joe Lloyd, where irrefutable DNA evidence was shamefully fabricated, leading to his unjust imprisonment for a staggering seventeen excruciating years for a crime he was incontrovertibly innocent of committing. It is crucial to elucidate that Lloyd was diagnosed with a severe case of schizophrenia at the time of the alleged offense. This condition undeniably impaired his cognitive capabilities and rendered him exceptionally vulnerable.

Nonetheless, he was mercilessly deemed fit for questioning and promptly manipulated by cunning investigators into yielding a false confession. Their unwavering desire to solve the case clouded their judgment and defied their ethical obligations. This harrowing illustration symbolizes yet another significant cause of wrongful conviction: the prevalence of false confessions and tragically self-incriminating guilty pleas, which are often extracted from susceptible and defenseless suspects who find themselves trapped in the intricate web of the justice system.

An all-too-disturbing example of this profoundly disturbing phenomenon can be found in the heart-wrenching case of Paul House, who also found himself trapped on death row, where his physical and mental disabilities were devastatingly instrumental in coercing him into delivering a false confession for the heinous murder and subsequent conviction of Carolyn Muncey. Astonishingly, House's disabilities proved to be decisive factors that cemented his role as an innocent man in a nightmarish ordeal that insidiously denied him the fundamental principles of truth, fairness, and justice.

Unmistakably, some suspects' vulnerabilities ensnare them within the devious sights of law enforcement agencies determined to swiftly conclude and resolve a case, transgressing ethical boundaries and compromising the integrity of the judicial process. Moreover, it is of paramount importance to duly acknowledge the pernicious role that systemic biases and deeply ingrained prejudices fortify within the ominous confines of the criminal justice system.

The disproportionately excessive targeting and profiling of specific communities that are based on uncontrollable factors such as race, ethnicity, or socioeconomic status undeniably exerts an undeniable influence on the outcome of investigations and trials. The alarming prevalence of implicit biases harbored by both law enforcement officials and jurors alike serves to perpetuate an environment that endorses the ill-treatment of suspects, ultimately culminating in the woefully predictable wave of wrongful convictions.

Genuine recognition and proactive mitigation of these profoundly ingrained biases emerge as imperatives that are pivotal to the ongoing crusade to forge a criminal justice system that is indisputably fair, impartial, and resolute in its unwavering pursuit of truth and justice. Additionally, the awe-inspiring advancements within forensic science and cutting-edge technology have undeniably shone an unyielding spotlight on the ubiquitous potential for errors, misconduct, and devastating breaches in the meticulous analysis and interpretation of evidence.

The alarming implications of faulty forensic techniques, ranging from the dubiously unreliable realm of fingerprint analysis to the starkly flawed arena of hair microscopy, reverberate as glaring examples of the obtrusive injustices that can be inflicted upon the lives of innocent individuals trapped in the clutches of an unforgiving and frequently flawed system.

The flagrant misuse or outright misinterpretation of forensic evidence invariably gives rise to a devastating cascade of consequences that perpetuates the infamous cycle of wrongful convictions, irreversibly shattering lives and mercilessly shredding the delicate fabric of trust that should inherently permeate the corridors of justice. Therefore, it is fundamentally imperative for law enforcement agencies, as well as the steadfast professionals operating within the realm of forensic science, to remain unyieldingly committed to the ever-evolving landscape of research, replete with best practices, and unwaveringly vigilant in their collective pursuit of excellence within their respective fields.

Furthermore, the profound role that inadequate legal representation and the overwhelming pressures associated with the profoundly adversarial nature of the criminal justice system manifest as equally formidable foes that should never be overlooked or relegated to insignificance.

Public defenders, who valiantly endeavor to safeguard the interests and liberties of individuals embroiled in the tumultuous maelstrom of the judicial process, frequently grapple with insurmountable caseloads, woefully limited resources, and insidiously suffocating time constraints that perennially undermine their capacity to conduct exhaustive and comprehensive investigations, as well as present a robust, unassailable defense that compassionately upholds their clients' rights and ensures an equitable legal process.

The insidious repercussions of insufficient legal representation emphatically resonate as catalysts that foster the vulnerability of defendants and exponentially increase the likelihood of deplorable wrongful convictions that irrevocably and irretrievably devastate lives.

Effectively addressing these deeply entrenched issues necessitates an unequivocal, collective effort by lawmakers, policymakers, legal professionals, and society. Genuine and resolute reform initiatives targeted at revitalizing the crippled landscape of the criminal justice system, bolstered by a multifaceted suite of well-calibrated safeguards designed to meticulously prevent misconduct, procuring adequate resources and support systems for defense attorneys, and unwaveringly championing education and awareness campaigns that shed light on the perils and injustices propagated by wrongful convictions, collectively represent crucial milestones on the arduous journey towards an equitable, compassionate, and unimpeachably just legal system that triumphantly embodies and upholds the principles of truth, fairness, and justice for all individuals who find themselves immersed within its formidable embrace. (Gould et al.2022)(Goswami and Goswami2022)(SCHETTERS et al., 2021)(Hession, 2020)(Gudjonsson, 2021)

12

Innocence Projects and DNA Evidence

The Innocence Project has brought to light the profound and far-reaching impact of wrongful convictions, unjustly robbing individuals of their freedom and tarnishing the integrity of the criminal justice system in the unwavering attention of the public eye. This awe-inspiring organization, serving as a beacon of hope and resilience, draws its name from the notion it embodies—innocence.

Operating as a national litigation organization within the borders of the United States, the Innocence Project remains unwaveringly committed to the noble cause of exonerating those who have been wrongfully convicted through the revolutionary means of DNA testing while simultaneously striving to reform the criminal justice system to safeguard against future injustices.

Over time, the Innocence Project has burgeoned into an extensive resource economy, propelling its transformative mission and unwavering dedication to seek truth and justice beyond the confines of a single organization.

Branching out across numerous states within the United States and even crossing international borders, this beacon of hope has sprouted offshoots in several other countries. These regional arms, shaped by the indomitable spirit of the Innocence Project, tirelessly toil towards two intertwined goals: championing the clearing of innocence, wiping the slate clean for those who have been erroneously condemned, and enacting comprehensive reform within the criminal justice system—two objectives that are inexorably intertwined in their urgency and necessity.

While the Innocence Project stands as a testament to the power of collaboration, unity, and the relentless pursuit of justice, it is by no means alone in its battle for truth and exoneration. Among the diverse innocence projects scattered throughout the nation, each fighting tenaciously to exonerate the wrongfully convicted, the Innocence Project shines as an inimitable force within the United States.

Its groundbreaking use of DNA evidence has revolutionized the very essence of these endeavors, bestowing upon them an indisputable method to establish and substantiate innocence. This monumental milestone waveringly heralds a new era in the fight for justice.

A powerful tool in affirming the guilt of those responsible for heinous acts. By harnessing the power of DNA, these tireless advocates can diligently traverse state and national databases, weaving together a web of unequivocal evidence that no guilty party can evade. Faced with such technological advancements, the criminal justice system gradually evolves, inching toward increased accuracy, fairness, and, above all, the preservation of justice.

As the Innocence Project and its vast network of allied innocence projects soldier on, the ripple effect of their audacious endeavors manifests in the immeasurable impact they have had—and continue to have—on countless lives. By striving to right the wrongs of the past while endeavoring to dismantle the systemic flaws within the criminal justice system, these beacons of hope ignite a fire within society, illuminating the path toward a future where innocence remains untarnished and justice thrives resplendently.

The Innocence Project's unwavering dedication to exonerating those wrongfully convicted and reforming the criminal justice system has struck a chord with people nationwide, resonating deeply within the hearts and minds of individuals who yearn for justice and fairness. As a result, the project has experienced tremendous growth, expanding its reach far beyond the borders of the United States. Its impact and influence have extended to numerous countries worldwide, spreading seeds of hope and resilience in the fight against wrongful convictions.

As the Innocence Project continues its vital work, assisted by its network of allied innocence projects, the impact of their audacious endeavors reverberates far and wide. Their tireless pursuit of justice has the power to transform countless lives, rectifying past wrongs and dismantling the systemic flaws ingrained within the criminal justice system. Through their unwavering dedication, these beacons of hope inspire society to envision a future where innocence is protected and justice thrives. Their efforts kindle a flame illuminating the path toward a more just and equitable world. (Norris et al.2020)(Norris et al.2020

The conventional methods of proving innocence often failed, with some cases of innocence being established after an execution. Even when convicts were spared from death, the evidence to prove their innocence was not always compelling.

Many innocent individuals were left to languish in prison, forgotten over time as witnesses forgot details, evidence was lost or destroyed, and the truth remained obscured. Despite countless efforts to prove innocence through traditional means, success was elusive.

The prevalence of individuals in US prisons claiming innocence has limited the success of traditional evidence. However, DNA evidence has been instrumental in freeing wrongfully convicted individuals and has the potential to prevent further miscarriages of justice. Legislation allowing convicts access to DNA testing has greatly aided in proving innocence and enhanced their claims' validity.

In addition to DNA evidence, advancements in forensic sciences such as anthropology, odontology, and fingerprint analysis have emerged as crucial tools in identifying and rectifying wrongful convictions. The development of digital forensics has also played a significant role in uncovering evidence that was previously inaccessible, offering immense potential to exonerate the innocent.

Furthermore, global networks and international cooperation have provided new avenues for seeking justice, emphasizing the global commitment to upholding justice and safeguarding the rights of the innocent. The modern world's interconnectedness has enabled information-sharing and collaboration among law enforcement agencies, legal professionals, and experts in various fields, transcending borders and working towards a common goal of fairness and innocence preservation.

In conclusion, while traditional evidence has often fallen short, the advancements in DNA technology, forensic sciences, digital forensics, and international collaboration offer renewed hope for those fighting to prove their innocence. The continuous development and application of these tools and techniques expand the possibilities in criminal justice, pushing us closer to a world where true justice prevails and innocence is always protected. Society's determination to uncover the truth and correct past injustices continues to evolve, promising a brighter and more just future for all. (Patel et al., 2021)(Saber et al., 2022)(Meintjes-Van and Dhliwayo2021)

Here would be an excellent time to discuss Compensation for the Wrongfully Convicted. Recompensing those unjustly imprisoned is a contentious and intricate matter that continues to provoke fervent discussions. In an ideal world, those wrongly confined should unquestionably receive some form of restitution for the profound injustice they have endured.

However, the practical execution of compensation presents numerous challenges and pitfalls that must be carefully navigated. The call for increased compensation for the wrongfully convicted has gained prominence, particularly in light of the release of several high-profile cases in the United States. The case of Glenn Ford, who spent an astonishing three decades on death row before being exonerated due to compelling new evidence, stands out as a prime example.

Astonishingly, Ford's initial compensation offer amounted to a mere

$20 and a bus ride home, underscoring the inadequacy of prevailing compensation measures. Nevertheless, whether Ford truly deserves compensation remains a subject of intense debate and dissent. An article published by CNN presented an intriguing perspective from one of the prosecutors involved in Ford's case, asserting, "Was he innocent of the murder of Harold Vincent? Absolutely not." This statement, while seemingly unequivocal, serves to highlight the complexity surrounding compensation for the wrongfully convicted.

Some argue that compensating individuals with a history of criminal activity perpetuates an unjust windfall, allowing them to exploit the system. Opponents of broad compensation policies also draw attention to the disturbing case of Alan Newton in 2014, who received a substantial sum of $18.5 million in compensation following his release from prison due to DNA evidence clearing him of a wrongful conviction. This exorbitant payout provoked widespread criticism, underscoring the potential for compensation mechanisms to go awry.

Moreover, it is crucial to consider the long-lasting impact of wrongful convictions on innocent individuals' lives. Beyond the immediate loss of freedom, there are profound psychological, emotional, and physical damages that cannot simply be resolved by monetary compensation alone. Rebuilding one's life after years spent behind bars is a monumental challenge that requires comprehensive support systems and resources.

While providing financial assistance is undoubtedly important, it should be accompanied by robust rehabilitation programs, access to education and employment opportunities, and mental health services tailored to the specific needs of the wrongfully convicted. Furthermore, the question of compensating the wrongfully convicted extends beyond individual cases.

It reflects the flaws within the justice system itself, highlighting the need for reforms to prevent future miscarriages of justice. By addressing systemic issues such as inadequate defense representation, biases within the legal system, and faulty forensic science practices, society can aspire to minimize the occurrence of wrongful convictions and subsequently reduce the need for extensive compensation.

To ensure fair and just compensation, it is essential to establish an impartial and transparent process for evaluating each case individually. A more accurate and thoughtful compensation can be determined by considering the severity and length of the wrongful imprisonment, the impact on the individual's life and livelihood, and any additional hardships endured during and after incarceration.

While it is challenging to strike a perfect balance between rectifying the harm inflicted upon innocent individuals and safeguarding against potential exploitation, a well-designed framework can guide the decision-making process and provide a measure of justice for those who have suffered immeasurable losses.

Ultimately, the issue of compensating the wrongfully convicted transcends simple monetary considerations. It necessitates a delicate balance between rectifying the immense harm inflicted upon innocent individuals and safeguarding against system exploitation. Without a robust framework, disputes, unrest, and controversial outcomes will persist, perpetuating the complex nature of this ongoing dilemma.

The road to justice for the wrongfully convicted may be fraught with challenges. Still, it is essential to strive for a system that not only acknowledges the injustice but takes concrete steps toward providing comprehensive support and restitution to those who have been unjustly imprisoned. Only by doing so can we hope to rectify the past, prevent future injustices, and move closer to a more equitable and just society for all. (Ryan Sr, 2020)(Keys2021)(Bright and Kwak, 2023)(Packrone2024)(Burke, 2023)

13

Ethical Considerations

This section will thoroughly analyze the numerous and diverse ethical considerations that necessitate careful and deep contemplation within the larger context of governments delegating their imprisonment services to external entities. It is of utmost importance and cannot be overstated how crucial it is to thoroughly and rigorously evaluate these ethical facets to guarantee the satisfactory and effective implementation of a fair and impartial system that highly values and respects human rights, actively promotes and enhances societal well-being, and engenders a profound sense of security, trust, and confidence among the general populace, thereby fostering an environment of harmonious coexistence and collective prosperity.

The lamentable loss of essential rights within our society undoubtedly sets the stage for the emergence of highly questionable and deeply troubling behavior. In a world where justice, equity, and fairness crumble under the weight of such catastrophic events, allowing such a grievous erosion of these cherished rights, we find ourselves venturing into uncharted territory where ethical boundaries are ruthlessly pushed to their limits. This distressing outcome not only significantly diminishes the very fabric of our democratic values but also tragically opens the floodgates for a deplorable disregard for the sacred principles that once served as the foundation of our civilization.

As our rights and freedoms are relentlessly stripped away, a grave consequence arises in a moral vacuum, where individuals feel justified in engaging in acts that were once universally condemned. Society must confront and bravely battle this unsettling reality that threatens to obliterate the essence of humanity. We must strive to prevent any further encroachment upon our cherished rights, for it is only through a relentless effort that we can hope to preserve the sanctity of our ethical compass.

With unwavering determination and resilience, we must resist the allure of improper conduct. Our collective voice must rise above the chaos, proclaiming that we will not allow the erosion of our fundamental rights to shape our destiny. When we stand united in the face of adversity, armed with the belief in the value of justice, fairness, and liberty, we can steer our society away from the treacherous precipice upon which it now teeters.

Let us not falter in pursuing a just society, for the stakes are too high and the consequences too severe. May our actions today safeguard the rights of generations yet to come, ensuring they are anchored by the unwavering principles that have defined us for centuries.

In these trying times, we must remember that the legacy of our ancestors hangs in the balance. We stand on the shoulders of those who fought for justice and freedom, and we must honor their sacrifice by preserving and expanding upon the rights they so valiantly battled for. The road ahead may be arduous and fraught with challenges and setbacks, but we must remain steadfast in our resolve to protect humanity's essence.

As we wage this vital battle against the forces of oppression, let us remember that the arc of history bends toward justice. We must ensure that this arc does not snap under the weight of tyranny and injustice. We have a collective responsibility to stand up for what is right, to demand that our voices be heard and our rights respected.

In this struggle, each of us has a role to play. We can make a difference through peaceful protest, advocacy, or raising awareness. We can push back against the encroachment upon our fundamental rights and reclaim the dignity and freedom that should be the birthright of every individual.

Let us not underestimate the power of unity. By coming together, amplifying our voices, and standing shoulder to shoulder, we can create a symphony of change that resonates throughout society. Let our actions serve as a testament to humanity's indomitable spirit and a beacon of hope for future generations.

May we never forget the price paid for the freedoms we hold dear. Let us honor the sacrifices of those who came before us by remaining vigilant guardians of justice and equality. Together, we build a legacy of resilience, compassion, and unwavering determination.

Let our resolve be unwavering in the face of adversity. Let our steps be firm and decisive in pursuing a just society. And let us leave no stone unturned in protecting our essential rights and preserving our democratic values. Our collective action can only shape a future of fairness, equality, and the unbreakable bond of shared humanity.

It was shockingly discovered in the vast land of Australia that contracts between the honorable state government and esteemed private companies contain perplexing clauses. These bewildering clauses explicitly demand that the government relentlessly strive to uphold a whopping 90% occupancy rate within the confines of private prisons. Theoretically, one could deduce that such a clause would obligate the government, under a binding contract, to foster high imprisonment rates actively.

The implications of this contractual obligation are profoundly disturbing, as they circumvent the fundamental notion of imprisonment solely as a means of punishment for criminal transgressions. Instead, it presents a disconcerting scenario where an individual's precious freedom is shamelessly infringed upon in service of ulterior motives and objectives.

Inexplicably, it is not beyond the realm of possibility that governments or even prison operators themselves may stoop to imprisoning innocent individuals who bear no criminal record whatsoever. This unjustifiable course of action might be justified under the flimsy guise of "preventative detention," which effectively masks the true objective of maintaining a steady prison population to reaping the economic benefits it bestows upon those involved. Such a distressing prospect should not be taken lightly, as it infringes upon the fabric of justice and the sanctity of civil liberties.

Conflicted interests can and do create the potential for injustice. It appears to be an almost foregone conclusion that conflicts of interest will inevitably arise when the provision of incarceration services is handed over to private entities, bringing with it a host of troubling implications.

The Bradley Report, a comprehensive examination of the Australian context, sheds light on a particularly distressing incident that unfolded within a US prison system. In this alarming example, young individuals were subjected to an egregiously flawed process wherein they were forced to endure what can only be described as a ridiculous kangaroo court. Astonishingly, these youths were deprived of the fundamental right to mount a defense, leaving them defenseless against an unjust verdict and ultimately finding themselves sentenced to imprisonment for transgressions that traditionally would not have warranted incarceration.

The deeply troubling nature of this case becomes even more evident upon the discovery that the presiding judge was, in fact, an employee of the very private prison firm that stood to profit from each conviction. Shockingly, it was revealed that this judge was clandestinely compensated a staggering sum of $2000 for every young life unjustly trapped in the clutches of the for-profit prison system.

While this particular instance may be extreme, its ramifications cannot be ignored. It forces us to confront critical inquiries concerning the judiciary's inherent susceptibility to corruption and the severe limitations imposed upon transparency and accountability in the governance of private correctional facilities.

The impact of such conflicts of interest and the erosion of justice they entail cannot be ignored, as they undermine the very fabric of our legal system and perpetuate a cycle of injustice. Hence, it becomes imperative for society to reevaluate the reliance on private entities within the realm of incarceration. This case serves as a chilling reminder of the dangers of allowing profit motives to overshadow the principles of fairness, equality, and rehabilitation.

The need for increased regulation, oversight, and transparency in private prisons is evident. These measures would ensure that the pursuit of justice remains uncompromised and untainted by vested interests. Only through these measures can we truly restore faith in our judicial system and ensure that no person, especially vulnerable young individuals, falls victim to the insidious intertwining of corporate profit and the deprivation of their fundamental rights.

The time for change is now, as we strive towards a more equitable and just society where the well-being and dignity of individuals take precedence over monetary gains. It is of utmost importance to recognize the dire consequences that arise when incarceration services are placed in the hands of private entities, as it invariably gives rise to conflicts of interest. These conflicts inevitably lead to many troubling implications that are detrimental to the fairness and integrity of the system. (Sterling, 2020)(Rakoff, 2021)(Messenger, 2021)

14

Morality vs. Profitability

The prison industry, driven by profit and fueled by unethical practices, deviates significantly from the principles that should underpin the justice system. For true justice to prevail, a definitive verdict must be rendered against those who have undeniably committed a crime, ensuring that the punishment's severity corresponds to the offense's gravity.

It is of utmost importance to acknowledge that the relentless quest for monetary gain must never eclipse the fundamental tenets of justice and morality, which necessitate the precise identification and just condemnation of individuals responsible for wrongdoing. Only by upholding these principles can we establish a system that truly serves the cause of justice and ensures a fair society for all.

The Vera Institute of Justice, an esteemed organization dedicated to advancing justice and reform within the criminal justice system, brings to light the critical issue of current policies that contribute to the swelling of prison populations and higher conviction rates. These policies specifically target drug offenders, creating an urgent need for reform to address the alarming increase in these numbers.

Shocking statistics from the year 2000 reveal that an astonishing 58%

of federal prisoners were convicted for drug offenses, marking a significant 27% increase since 1986. These figures raise important questions about the effectiveness and consequences of drug prohibition.

Without a doubt, the war on drugs has proven to be a profit-driven policy, resulting in severe social repercussions. In recent years, the focus on intensified policing and the implementation of harsh, inflexible mandatory sentencing has led to a surge in convictions and arrest rates. Paradoxically, these efforts have failed to produce any significant decrease in drug abuse within the United States. A striking example of this paradox is the controversial Rockefeller Drug Laws enacted in the 1970s.

In 2002, a comprehensive study shed light on the profound impact of drug law reforms. These reforms uncovered a startling revelation: the rate at which criminals were being released on parole had doubled. Consequently, it became evident that the changes in legislation did not result in a corresponding increase in the number of individuals involved in drug offenses. Instead, these reforms unintentionally led to a surge in incarceration rates, primarily driven by heightened conviction rates and lengthy sentences.

The consequences of these policies stretch far beyond the individuals imprisoned, as families and communities disproportionately affected by these highly punitive measures continue to face long-lasting repercussions, perpetuating a cycle of systemic inequality.

The complex interplay between policy, criminal justice, and drug offenses necessitates a comprehensive and multifaceted approach to reform. By acknowledging current policies' limitations and counterproductive outcomes, society can strive towards implementing efficient, equitable, and evidence-based solutions.

Policymakers and stakeholders must collaborate to foster restorative justice practices that prioritize rehabilitation and community reintegration and address the root causes of drug abuse. The thought-provoking analysis conducted by the Vera Institute of Justice urges us to reassess existing paradigms and embark on a transformative journey toward achieving genuine justice and rehabilitation within our criminal justice system. This calls for meaningful investments in education, mental health services, harm reduction strategies, and social support systems that empower individuals to break free from the cycle of addiction and crime.

Recognizing the intersections of systemic racism, socioeconomic disparities, and drug policy is essential to ensuring that any reform efforts are grounded in principles of equity and social justice. By addressing the underlying social determinants that contribute to drug abuse and criminal behavior, we can work towards preventing the over-policing and over-incarceration of marginalized communities. The research and advocacy provided by the Vera Institute of Justice offer a framework for a more compassionate and practical approach to criminal justice reform.

In conclusion, the expansion of the provided text underscores the urgent need for reform in drug policies and the criminal justice system as a whole. It emphasizes the importance of evidence-based solutions, restorative practices, and addressing the root causes of drug abuse. By embarking on a transformative journey towards genuine justice and rehabilitation, society has the potential to create a more equitable and inclusive system that uplifts individuals and communities. The analysis conducted by the Vera Institute of Justice serves as a powerful call to action, urging us to challenge existing paradigms and work towards a society where justice is indeed served. (Messmore, 2020)(Durose and Antenangeli2021)(Heimer et al.2023)(Cochran et al.2021)

15

Human Rights and Dignity of the Incarcerated

Following conviction and imprisonment, there remains a matter of public perception that when a given convict has been unequivocally proven innocent after the fact or new exculpating evidence has come to light that would indisputably acquit the convict of the crime upon which he was unjustly convicted, that the individual has, in some manner, been provided with the true essence of justice upon the undeniable and irrefutable exoneration from his wrongful conviction.

However, it is essential to recognize that this mere appearance of justice can be highly deceptive, for in reality, the exoneration of a convict from a crime that he did not commit does not in any way constitute a justice that can be considered as a fair and moral counterpart to the preceding wrongful conviction (Bedau, 1997). The profound damage inflicted by a grievous miscarriage of justice extends far beyond the alleviation of guilt, as it encompasses the irreparable loss of potential, future, freedom years, or even years of life, which can never be restored or traded for even the most substantial or extended monetary compensation, regardless of any rate that may try to equate it to the immeasurable value of a single human life (Radelet, L. & Zsembik, B 1993).

It is an unfortunate reality that the measures implemented to enhance justice for wrongful convictions often fall woefully short in terms of allocating sufficient resources to provide adequate justice for former inmates who have been victims of egregious wrongful convictions. Despite the logical and moral implications that should be inherent in such cases, high courts and legislative bodies have historically displayed a significant hesitancy to establish past conviction as an unequivocal barrier for the retrial of a wrongfully accused crime.

This unwillingness creates a profoundly unjust and inequitable situation where the wrongfully convicted individuals must tirelessly and laboriously pursue their release through lengthy and arduous legal avenues, often encountering numerous rejections when seeking resources and aid that could potentially make the pivotal difference between a conviction and an acquittal (Huff, 2004; Findley, 1987).

As the current state of affairs stands, the majority of convicts who are later exonerated through the arduous postconviction proceedings or other means are effectively left to navigate their path of restoration within a society that has grievously wronged them, if they are fortunate enough to find any semblance of restoration at all. When a convict has been proven innocent or new evidence emerges to acquit them, there is a public perception that justice has been served. However, this perception is deceptive.

These wrongfully convicted individuals must navigate a labyrinthine system, fighting against the odds to prove their innocence and regain their rightful place in society. The journey for exoneration is treacherous, filled with obstacles and setbacks that test their resolve and resilience. Yet, despite the glaring injustices inflicted upon them, they persist, fuelled by a deep-seated belief in their own innocence and a fervent desire to reclaim their stolen years.

Their battles are fought in the courtroom and in the court of public opinion, where skepticism and doubt can cast a long shadow over their quest for redemption. Society, too, bears a burden - a burden of introspection and accountability for the wrongful convictions that stain its reputation. It must confront its own fallibility and acknowledge the devastating impact of its failures.

Ultimately, the accurate measure of justice lies not in an exoneration's empty words but in the subsequent transformative actions. It is a call for reform, reparation, and a systematic change that will prevent the recurrence of such grave miscarriages of justice. It is a demand for a society that values truth, fairness, and preserving human dignity above all else. Only then can the wounds inflicted by wrongful convictions begin to heal, and the scars of injustice fade into the annals of history.

16

Reforming the Prison System

The ever-growing predicament of overcrowded prisons has ascended to a degree of utmost significance and gravity, and policymakers must embark upon a comprehensive and all-encompassing strategy to completely revitalize and overhaul the prison system. In an earnest endeavor to confront the quandary of overly excessive incarceration rates and its detrimentally adverse impact on society as a cohesive whole, the government must allocate substantial resources towards the implantation and execution of alternative modes of punishment for non-violent offenders and, therefore, considerably reduce the duration of prison sentences for these individuals.

Moreover, there exists an urgent and potentially life-altering necessity to reevaluate the existing policies concerning drug-related offenses diligently and, in a more compassionate and conscientious approach, endeavor to liberate those who have been unjustly convicted from their cruel incarcerations. Furthermore, it is paramount to focus concerted efforts on formulating and developing pioneering crime prevention techniques that effectively and efficiently curb the occurrence and prevalence of criminal activities.

Only by substantially deploying these multifaceted measures can we hope to alleviate the excessive strain plaguing our prison system and foster a more equitable, just, and harmonious society. Imprisoning non-violent offenders places an unnecessary and heavy burden on the already strained prison system, which is struggling to cope with overcrowding and limited resources.

Instead, implementing alternatives such as house arrest or restriction of movement would address the issue and maintain the offender's connection to the community. By allowing them to continue working and supporting their families, we provide a more effective form of punishment and reduce the financial burden on taxpayers. Additionally, these alternative methods promote the rehabilitation and reintegration of non-violent offenders into society, ensuring their successful transition back to a law-abiding lifestyle.

Implementing house arrest or restriction of movement for nonviolent offenders offers numerous advantages. Not only does it enable the offender to maintain their employment and contribute to the economy, but it also facilitates their rehabilitation and reintegration into society. By retaining ties with their families and communities, these offenders are more likely to develop a sense of responsibility and accountability, which can significantly reduce the likelihood of reoffending. Moreover, utilizing these alternatives takes a proactive approach by addressing the root causes of criminal behavior while minimizing the financial strain on the corrections system, allowing for a more efficient use of resources.

In addition to house arrest, probation is another viable alternative for nonviolent offenders. Although it does not confine the individual, probation imposes strict conditions and restrictions that serve as punishment. This method holds the offender accountable for their actions and provides the necessary structure and guidance for their successful reintegration. Through close monitoring of their behavior and progress, probation officers can ensure compliance and provide support where required, effectively reducing the risk of recidivism and promoting a safe and secure society.

It is crucial to recognize that most prisoners will eventually be released back into society. Consequently, it is imperative to prioritize their successful reintegration and reduce the barriers they face, particularly regarding employment. A criminal record can severely limit opportunities for former prisoners, making it challenging to acquire gainful employment and sustain a stable life.

By utilizing alternatives to incarceration for non-violent offenders, such as house arrest and probation, we give them a chance to rebuild their lives and contribute positively to society. This enhances public safety and fosters a sense of empowerment and self-worth among these individuals, increasing their chances of long-term success and reducing re-offense rates.

Moreover, the current treatment of prisoners with drug offenses requires an immediate change. Instead of mere incarceration without addressing the underlying issues, it is essential to implement comprehensive treatment programs. These programs can help individuals overcome addiction, addressing the root causes of their criminal behavior rather than compounding the problem through imprisonment alone.

By providing the necessary support and resources, we can break the cycle of drug-related offenses and assist offenders in regaining control of their lives. This approach contributes to public health and safety and promotes a compassionate and humane society that values rehabilitation and second chances.

In conclusion, the outdated practice of imprisoning non-violent offenders imposes a significant burden on the prison system while offering limited benefits to society. Alternatives such as house arrest, restriction of movement, and probation provide more effective forms of punishment that not only hold offenders accountable but also facilitate their reintegration into the community. By prioritizing rehabilitation and addressing the underlying issues, we can enhance public safety, reduce recidivism rates, and alleviate the strain on the corrections system. It is time to embrace progressive and cost-effective approaches while ensuring the successful reintegration of individuals into society, creating a safer and more inclusive future for all. (Bailey, 2022)(Razali et al.2021)(WALKER, 2024)

Now more than ever, we need Sentencing Reforms and Alternatives to Incarceration. One highly successful alternative to incarceration is electronic monitoring, which provides offenders with the opportunity to serve their sentences from the comfort of their own homes while being closely monitored by probation officials.

Mandarin argues that electronic monitoring (EM) can be a valuable tool for low-risk offenders and in cases involving non-violent crimes. According to him, the success of the electronic monitoring business primarily stems from its cost-effectiveness compared to imprisonment. Astonishingly, a comprehensive study conducted in California revealed that the daily cost of monitoring an offender on EM was a mere $9.38, starkly contrasting to the hefty $78.95 per day required to incarcerate an offender. It is evident that EM possesses various advantages; however, one can argue that it may not be a suitable punishment for the most heinous crime, like murder.

In the United Kingdom, the principal guiding principle for sentencing revolves around ensuring that the punishment matches the gravity of the crime committed. Consequently, electronic monitoring may be perceived as a lenient option, lacking the adequate severity required to punish crimes like murder. This is particularly noteworthy with the HM Government's contentious "indeterminate sentencing" approach for public protection, implemented in 2003. Under this scheme, offenders can potentially be incarcerated indefinitely until their release is deemed safe. Historically, this has resulted in mandatory life sentences for grave offenses such as murder. Compared to these robust sentencing practices, electronic monitoring is not considered a viable alternative, and the cost-effectiveness boasted earlier loses its relevance in this context.

However, it is essential to acknowledge that electronic monitoring can still play a significant role in the criminal justice system. For instance, it can be an effective measure for less severe offenses, allowing offenders to maintain ties with their families, continue their employment, and contribute to society in a controlled manner. Additionally, EM can alleviate the issue of prison overcrowding, reducing the strain on correctional facilities and the associated costs. By diverting low-risk offenders from incarceration to electronic monitoring, resources can be freed up to focus on those who pose a higher risk to public safety.

Moreover, technological advancements have led to more sophisticated electronic monitoring systems. For example, GPS tracking devices can provide real-time data on an offender's location, ensuring compliance with court-ordered restrictions. This enhances public safety by allowing authorities to intervene promptly in case of violations. Furthermore, EM can be combined with rehabilitative programs to address the underlying causes of criminal behavior, promoting the successful reintegration of offenders into society.

In conclusion, while electronic monitoring may not be suitable for the most heinous crimes, it offers a viable and cost-effective alternative to traditional incarceration for low-risk offenders. By carefully implementing and utilizing technologies such as GPS tracking, electronic monitoring can contribute to maintaining public safety while addressing issues such as prison overcrowding. Policymakers must consider the specific circumstances of each case and the impact of different sentencing options to make informed decisions that balance punishment, rehabilitation, and societal well-being. (Klein Haneveld, 2022)

Creating or modifying sentences is another highly recommended and impactful approach to diminishing the size of the prison population and shifting the focus away from the mere incarceration of offenders. By implementing sentence modification techniques, we can address the issue of overcrowding in prisons and move towards a more rehabilitative justice system. A noteworthy illustration of the effectiveness of sentence modification can be observed in the drug policies implemented in the United States, where significant changes have been made to combat the detrimental effects of the war on drugs.

The war on drugs policies, which have widely been regarded as a failure, has undeniably resulted in a detrimental effect: the overwhelming overcrowding of prisons due to the imprisonment of drug offenders. It is crucial to note that minimum sentences play a substantial role in exacerbating this issue since they compel judges to incarcerate offenders, even in instances where the severity, magnitude, and weight of the sentence do not align with the gravity of the offense committed. This unjust practice has led to an unjustifiably high number of individuals serving lengthy prison terms for non-violent drug offenses.

Conversely, countries such as Canada and the Netherlands have taken progressive strides by adopting a more lenient, compassionate, and forward-thinking approach to sentencing policies for drug offenders. This commendable shift represents a form of decriminalization, emphasizing the fact that individuals convicted of drug offenses are no longer automatically subjected to imprisonment. In these countries, the focus has shifted towards comprehensive rehabilitation programs, providing robust support services, and addressing the underlying issues that contribute to drug addiction.

Furthermore, it is worth mentioning that mandatory minimum sentences for cannabis offenses were abolished in the Netherlands as early as 1996. This highly progressive and enlightened decision recognizes that lengthy prison terms are not the solution to effectively addressing drug-related issues. By removing these mandatory minimum sentences, the Netherlands has been able to effectively allocate substantial resources towards evidence-based rehabilitation programs, holistic community support systems, and comprehensive treatment options for individuals struggling with drug addiction.

Implementing problem-solving courts is an additional noteworthy avenue for sentence creation/modification. These specialized courts prioritize addressing offenders' underlying issues and challenges instead of resorting to simple punitive measures such as incarceration. By focusing on rehabilitation and providing access to necessary support systems, problem-solving courts have proven remarkably effective in reducing recidivism rates and promoting positive social reintegration.

Notably, drug courts serve as a prominent exemplification and manifestation of problem-solving courts in action, as they prioritize rehabilitating drug addicts rather than subjecting them to the cold confines of imprisonment. These courts provide individuals with the invaluable opportunity to receive tailored treatment plans, specialized counseling, and comprehensive support systems to overcome their addiction and reintegrate successfully into society as productive members. By addressing the root causes of drug addiction, these courts aim to decisively break the multigenerational cycle of substance abuse and recurring criminal behavior.

Admittedly, effecting significant and transformative changes to sentencing policies and successfully implementing programs like problem-solving courts may require a considerable and ambitious overhaul of the current system. However, the immense benefits of fully embracing, adopting, and integrating these alternative methods cannot be understated.

By consciously shifting our collective focus towards a more empathetic, rehabilitative, and holistic approach and diligently addressing the underlying societal issues that contribute to crime, we have the inherent ability and profound potential to build a more equitable, just, and compassionate justice system that reduces the likelihood of individuals being unjustly subjected to long-term incarceration and ultimately, substantially decreases the devastating rate of recidivism.

Suggestion: To effectively address the issue at hand and achieve meaningful outcomes, like expanding rehabilitation and Reentry Programs, it is highly recommended that policymakers and relevant authorities allocate substantial additional financial resources to enhance interstate transfer of supervision. This will ensure a seamless process and promote the well-being of individuals under parole by facilitating family reunification and ensuring long-term stability.

It is of utmost importance to provide parole officers with comprehensive guidance to assist them in their crucial role. This guidance should cover various aspects of facilitating the family reunification process, including assistance in navigating legal requirements, connecting families with necessary resources, and offering support in addressing any potential challenges that may arise. By equipping parole officers with the necessary tools and knowledge, they can effectively guide and support ex-offenders and their families during this critical period.

Moreover, it is imperative to establish and implement well-designed programs and initiatives that focus on reuniting children with their parents who are ex-offenders. These programs should be tailored to meet the specific needs and circumstances of the families involved. Providing comprehensive support and assistance to parents and children is essential for cultivating positive and nurturing parenting skills.

By providing parenting education, counseling services, and access to community resources, ex-offenders can have the necessary support to successfully reintegrate into society while creating a healthy and secure environment for their children's growth and development. This approach ensures that essential support and assistance are provided to cultivate positive parenting skills, ultimately fostering a healthy and secure environment for children's growth and development.

The destruction of family bonds by the criminal justice system is a distressingly common occurrence. The repercussions of children growing up without a parent and parents missing out on their child's formative years are genuinely unimaginable and often irreversible. Child development experts vehemently argue that active and involved parenting profoundly influences a child's social, emotional, and cognitive development.

However, incarceration makes active parenting impossible for prisoners, leaving many with little to no guidance or support upon release on how to effectively resume their role as a parent and rebuild that crucial parent-child relationship. Furthermore, suppose an ex-offender is violated and sent back to prison on a mere technicality. In that case, their attempts to reconnect with their family are likely to be abruptly halted, further straining the already fragile family unit and perpetuating a cycle of despair and disconnection.

Despite overwhelming evidence showing that stable family bonds greatly enhance an offender's chances of successfully reintegrating into society and reducing the risk of recidivism, the current parole system offers minimal opportunities for parolees to rebuild and maintain healthy family relationships. The lack of resources and support dedicated to family reunification is a glaring oversight within our criminal justice system. We must recognize the vital role of family reunification in fostering a sense of purpose, stability, and belonging for ex-offenders.

To address this critical issue, we must prioritize family reunification and actively support parolees in rebuilding and maintaining stable family bonds. By investing in comprehensive programs and services that address the unique challenges faced by ex-offenders as they transition back into society, we can pave the way for a more compassionate and effective criminal justice system. These programs should include parent-child bonding interventions, marriage and family counseling, vocational training, and mentoring programs specifically tailored to the needs of ex-offenders and their families.

Moreover, we must establish proactive measures to prevent unnecessary disruptions in family bonds. This includes implementing policies that promote fair and just decision-making regarding parole violations and ensuring that ex-offenders are not unjustly sent back to prison for minor infractions. Instead, we should focus on providing alternative sanctions and support services that enable individuals to address the root causes of their behavior while staying connected with their loved ones.

The well-being and successful reintegration of ex-offenders into their families, communities, and society at large depend on urgent action to ensure that they have the opportunity to embark on a path free from crime and full of hope for a brighter future. By addressing the underlying issues that contribute to family separation and actively working towards building stronger family bonds, we can create a criminal justice system that puts compassion, rehabilitation, and long-term positive outcomes at its core. Only then can we genuinely support ex-offenders journey toward lasting transformation and contribute to safer, more cohesive communities. (Kaeble and Alper, 2020)(Robson et al.2020)(Wiggins et al.2022)

Any substantial change in the conditions described above must involve Addressing Systemic Issues and Bias, far more than merely adjusting law enforcement officers' or prosecutors' beliefs and behaviors. As numerous astute and diligent observers have rightly noted, bias against certain defendants and certain classes of crime is deeply rooted and ingrained within the legal consciousness and culture.

It is an undeniable truth that such discrimination is not only accelerated or perpetuated but also fortified by public opinion, often serving as a catalyst for egregious injustice. It is a disheartening and distressing reality to witness prosecutors entrusted with upholding justice willingly forsaking their ethical obligations and shamelessly manipulating their role, particularly in cases where the public widely disliked or disdained defendants and offenses.

This disconcerting and alarming trend has been empirically examined and proven, as incontrovertibly demonstrated by William J. Bowers and his esteemed colleagues in their extensive research on capital sentencing in the state of Georgia. Their meticulous and comprehensive findings unequivocally reveal that the outcome and direction of a trial are essentially preordained and heavily influenced by prevailing public attitudes.

Moreover, the likelihood of securing a guilty verdict, be it through fair or foul means, substantially increases when society seeks stringent retribution for the victim and consistently undervalues and trivializes the profound gravity of the crime committed. The existence and propagation of pervasive and deeply ingrained stereotypes only exacerbate the already dire situation, further entwining and entrenching the deeply rooted biases within the intricate fabric of the legal system.

This intricate and pernicious bias meticulously molds the course of a trial. It gravely impacts the probable outcome for individuals who are wrongly accused and who happen to belong to a corresponding race, class, or ethnic background.

Given the deep-seated influence of prevailing attitudes within the community and the ingrained mindset of officials carefully chosen from the same community, it is highly improbable to anticipate the complete eradication of bias. Merely substituting white officials with black ones or male officials with middle-class female ones does not offer a foolproof guarantee of a groundbreaking change in the existing discriminatory policies and practices.

Therefore, it becomes incredibly important to undertake a thorough cleansing and reevaluation of the legal system to address this profoundly concerning issue comprehensively. This multifaceted approach involves a meticulous reexamination of cases influenced by biased attitudes and reforming the modes of adjudication that perpetuate discrimination. By embracing and implementing these indispensable measures, we can effectively mitigate the deleterious impact of biased attitudes on our legal system and recognize the urgent need for transformative change.

A complete and comprehensive overhaul is essential for uprooting the profoundly ingrained biases that have plagued our legal system for far too long. It is imperative to thoroughly challenge the prevailing practices that have perpetuated discrimination and prejudice. By undertaking a systematic and in-depth analysis, we can uncover the potential biases that have seeped into the fabric of our legal institutions.

By adopting these necessary measures, we can collectively work towards mitigating and reducing the pervasive and damaging impact that biased attitudes have had on our legal system. This process will not be easy, nor will it be without resistance. However, our moral imperative is to confront these issues head-on and strive for a legal system that upholds the principles of fairness, equality, and justice for all. Only through comprehensive reform can we aspire to build a society where bias holds no dominion and where the rule of law reigns supreme.

In recent years, there has been a significant increase in the willingness to try and achieve this end by including federal oversight and litigation. This strategy has proven to be particularly influential when considering the death penalty. In the groundbreaking case of Furman v. Georgia, the Supreme Court observed that the death penalty had frequently been imposed arbitrarily and capriciously, causing concerns among legal scholars and human rights activists. While the Justices had differing opinions on whether the abolition of this penalty was the sole solution, it became evident that complete abolition would be unattainable due to the prevailing public opinion in most states and the political complexity surrounding the issue.

Thus, a novel alternative approach was adopted – diligent monitoring of the administration of the death penalty at the state level. The objective was to determine whether it could be implemented in a manner that upholds the principles of fairness and consistency as enshrined in the Eighth and Fourteenth Amendments of the United States Constitution.

This process involved comprehensive assessments of each state's capital punishment system, including gathering empirical data, conducting extensive research on legal precedents and international standards related to the death penalty, and engaging in dialogues with various stakeholders, such as lawmakers, legal professionals, and civil society organizations.

The findings of these meticulous examinations revealed significant disparities and discrepancies in the application of the death penalty across different jurisdictions. In states where substantial evidence is found to support the discriminatory implementation of the death penalty, appropriate injunctive relief will be enacted, preventing any further capital prosecutions for reasons that are void of any legitimate basis. These injunctions will serve as crucial safeguards, ensuring that individuals are not unjustly sentenced to death based on arbitrary factors such as race, socioeconomic status, or geographic location.

The success of this approach would undoubtedly signify a significant stride in the pursuit of eliminating the negative impacts of stereotypes and discriminatory beliefs that pervade the issuing of penal sanctions. It would reinforce the principle that every individual's right to life should be protected and respected, irrespective of their background or circumstances. By fostering a more equitable and just criminal justice system, the diligent monitoring of the death penalty at the state level aims to address the flaws and biases within the current system and restore public trust and confidence in the fairness of the legal process.

Moving forward, the ongoing dedication to federal oversight and litigation in matters about the death penalty is of paramount importance. Implementing such monitoring mechanisms must remain robust and comprehensive, ensuring that no individual falls victim to a system plagued by prejudice and inconsistency. By critically examining the administration of capital punishment and holding states accountable for any violations of constitutional rights, we can strive toward a future where the principles of fairness, justice, and human rights prevail over arbitrary and discriminatory practices. We can achieve a more just and enlightened society through these concerted efforts.(Sabriseilabi et al., 2022)(Itskovich et al., 2023)(Westbrook, 2023)

Conclusion

Politicians vehemently deny the shift in the legal system from upholding justice and service to a more populist approach focused on addressing new social threats. Emphasis is now placed on punitive containment and control rather than rehabilitation or protection as communities' various manifestations of threats are defined.

However, the public will eventually realize that pursuing these crime control philosophies is too expensive in terms of financial resources and the impact on individual liberties. The legal system's ability to self-correct is fundamental to maintaining equilibrium and ensuring the protection of all citizens despite being afflicted by rights violations.

Increased scrutiny from the public and media has brought significant attention to the plights of the wrongfully convicted, potentially triggering a powerful backlash against the continued assault on the accused's rights and dignity. The people's growing awareness and outrage may eventually lead to a formidable demand for reforms prioritizing fairness, rehabilitation, and the preservation of civil liberties.

The legal system must recognize the importance of safeguarding the rights of every individual, preserving the integrity of justice, and upholding the values upon which society is built. Together, as a collective voice, we can strive for a legal system that truly serves and protects, steering away from the dangerous path of punishment and condemnation.

It is no longer enough to work exclusively towards reactive measures on individual instances of injustice. To truly eradicate wrongful convictions, an urgent and imperative shift must occur, placing the prevention of such injustices at the forefront of the innocence movement. Comprehensive and multifaceted measures must be implemented to address and mitigate the societal and state factors that give rise to wrongful convictions in the first place.

Regardless of one's race, class, or political stance, an increasing number of people now recognize that the current practical punitive crime control measures are inadequate and have tragically resulted in the conviction of innocent individuals. Thus, significant changes must be made, surpassing mere cosmetic adjustments. At the same time, subjects of ongoing dialogue and debate, the extent and precise implementation methods must be approached with an unwavering commitment to uprooting the systemic flaws ingrained in our criminal justice system.as well as the extent and precise implementation methods,

As a critical force in effecting change, the innocence movement is undoubtedly profoundly intertwined with the core principles of reform embedded within the criminal justice system. Its primary objective is leveraging comprehensive rule reforms to effectively restrict discretion at every stage of a criminal case, from the initial arrest to the subsequent appeal process.

By prioritizing the reduction of discretionary decision-making, the Innocence movement aims to establish a fairer and more equitable system that upholds justice and safeguards the rights of all individuals involved. This necessitates substantive alterations to the current practices and ideologies that perpetuate wrongful convictions, ensuring that no innocent person falls victim to the system's faults.

The Innocence movement must engage in persistent discourse and cooperation with relevant stakeholders, including lawmakers, legal professionals, and advocacy groups to achieve these goals. This collaborative effort can generate comprehensive legislative reforms that prioritize the protection of the innocent and significantly diminish the likelihood of wrongful convictions. Additionally, fostering public awareness and education about the flaws within the criminal justice system is crucial.

By amplifying the voices and experiences of those who have suffered from wrongful convictions and highlighting the inherent biases and shortcomings in the current framework, society as a whole can be galvanized to demand change and support the innocence movement's endeavors.

Moreover, the Innocence Movement must advocate for proactive measures holistically addressing the underlying factors contributing to wrongful convictions. This includes enhanced law enforcement training to minimize errors and biases, improved forensic science techniques to ensure accurate evidence analysis, and increased access to quality legal representation for marginalized communities.

Moreover, robust mechanisms for reviewing and reevaluating past convictions are essential. These mechanisms could allow for the potential discovery of new evidence or the recognition of procedural errors that may have led to wrongful outcomes. The Innocence movement can pave the way for a more just and fair society by challenging the status quo and promoting continuous improvements.

In conclusion, the fight against wrongful conviction requires a comprehensive and unwavering commitment to reform. The Innocence movement must lead the charge in dismantling the systemic flaws perpetuating injustice, working towards a criminal justice system prioritizing prevention over reactionary measures. Through collaborative efforts, public education, legislative reforms, and proactive measures, the Innocence Movement can strive towards a future where the conviction of innocent individuals becomes rare and regrettable. Let us unite in this endeavor, for justice demands nothing less.

References:

Foss, J. "The Failings and Implications of the Prison Litigation Reform Act of 1995." (2023). uoregon.edu

Reilly, S. B. "Where Is the Strike Zone? Arguing for a Uniformly Narrow Interpretation of the Prison Litigation Reform Act's Three Strikes Rule." Emory LJ (2020). emory.edu

Appleman, L. I. "Bloody Lucre: Carceral Labor and Prison Profit." Wis. L. REv. (2022). wisc.edu

Reiman, J. and Leighton, P. "The rich get richer and the poor get prison: Thinking critically about class and criminal justice." (2020). losrios.edu

Young, E. "Forever Prisoners: How the United States Made the World's Largest Immigrant Detention System." (2020). [HTML]

Raher, S. "The company store and the literally captive market: Consumer law in prisons and jails." Hastings Race & Poverty LJ (2020). uclawsf.edu

Wooldredge, J. "Prison culture, management, and in-prison violence." Annual Review of Criminology (2020). archive.org

Neal, Derek A., and Armin Rick. "The Role of Policy in Prison Growth and Decline." University of Chicago, Becker Friedman Institute for Economics Working Paper 2023-150 (2023). uchicago.edu

Zimring, F. E. "The insidious momentum of American mass incarceration." (2020). [HTML]

Eubank, N. and Fresh, A. "Enfranchisement and incarceration after the 1965 Voting Rights Act." American Political Science Review (2022). cambridge.org

Brophy, M., Pérez-Luño, A., and Cooney, T. M. "Competency-based training within the prison system: enhancing the likelihood of entrepreneurial activity upon release." Journal of Education and ... (2024). tandfonline.com

Towne, Katelynn, Michael Campagna, Ryan Spohn, and Amber Richey. "“Put it in your toolbox”: How vocational programs support formerly incarcerated persons through reentry." Crime & Delinquency 69, no. 2 (2023): 316-341. unomaha.edu

Dee, D. C. "A 50-Year Systematic Analysis of US Drug Enforcement Legislation: Identifying Intended and Unintended Outcomes." (2021). [HTML]

Carl, John. "Mass Incarceration and For-Profit Prisons." Handbook of Forensic Social Work: Theory, Policy, and Fields of Practice (2024): 205. [HTML]

Kaeble, D. "Probation and parole in the United States, 2020." (2021). antonio-casella.eu

Baker, Jeffrey R. "Legal Foundations of the Business of Incarceration." The BUSINESS OF INCARCERATION: THEOLOGICAL AND ETHICAL REFLECTIONS ON THE PRISON-INDUSTRIAL COMPLEX (Cascade, Forthcoming) (2022). [HTML]

Zhang, Y. "Did the prison industrial complex deliver on its promise? Prison proliferation and employment in rural America." The British Journal of Criminology (2024). [HTML]

Soto, O. F. "La Mafia Global: Global Capitalism and the Struggle Against Hyper-Incarceration." (2023). escholarship.org

Cassady, H. M. "A global pandemic meets a prison system plagued with constitutional violations: COVID-19 in Alabama prisons." Cumb. L. Rev. (2022). [HTML]

Pfaff, J. F. "The incentives of private prisons." Ariz. St. LJ (2020). fordham.edu

Gunderson, A. "Why do states privatize their prisons? The unintended consequences of inmate litigation." Perspectives on Politics (2022). [HTML]

Appleman, L. I. "The treatment-industrial complex: Alternative corrections, private prison companies, and criminal justice debt." Harv. CR-CLL Rev. (2020). prisonlegalnews.org

Swanson, J. and Katzenstein, M. F. "Turning over the keys: Public prisons, private equity, and the normalization of markets behind bars." Perspectives on Politics (2021). [HTML]

Phillips, G. "Private Prison Blues: The Effect of Private Prisons on Recidivism Rates and State Outcomes." (2022). gracenphillips.com

Moranelli, R. A. "An Investigation Into the Collaboration of Mental Health and Social Worker Services with the Criminal Justice System." (2021). ohiolink.edu

Vollinger, L. and Campbell, R. "Youth service provision and coordination among members of a regional human trafficking task force." Journal of Interpersonal Violence (2022). [HTML]

Levin, B. "After the criminal justice system." Wash. L. Rev. (2023). wustl.edu

Grunwald, B. "Toward an Optimal Decarceration Strategy." Stan. L. & Pol'y Rev. (2022). stanford.edu

Rose, E. K. and Shem-Tov, Y. "How does incarceration affect reoffending? estimating the dose-response function." Journal of Political Economy (2021). github.io

Galle, B. "The Economic Case for Rewards Over Imprisonment." Ind. LJ (2020). indiana.edu

Freeman, J. and Jacobs, S. "Structural Deregulation." Harv. L. Rev. (2021). colorado.edu

Hollis-Brusky, A. and Wilson, J. C. "Separate but faithful: the Christian Right's radical struggle to transform law & legal culture." (2020). [HTML]

Black, D. W. "Schoolhouse burning: Public education and the assault on American democracy." (2020). [HTML]

Clark, L. T. B. "Whose child is this? Education, property, and belonging." Colum. L. Rev. (2023). columbialawreview.org

Driver, J. "Three Hail Marys: Carson, Kennedy, and the Fractured Détente over Religion and Education." Harv. L. Rev. (2022). yale.edu

Eren, C. P. "Reform Nation: The First Step Act and the Movement to End Mass Incarceration." (2023). [HTML]

Park, J. "US Immigration Politics, Sanctions Threats and Private Prison Corporations' Stock Market Values." The British Journal of Criminology (2023). [HTML]

Anzalone, N. "Should Private Prisons in the US be Abolished." (2021). molloy.edu

Yamahiro, Hana, and Luna Garzón-Montano. "A Mirage, Not a Movement: The Misguided Enterprise of Progressive Prosecution." NYU REV. L. & SOC. CHANGE 46 (2022): 130-134. socialchangenyu.com

Turner, Jennifer, Mariana Olaizola Rosenblat, Nino Guruli, Claudia Flores, Sophie Desch, Katya El Tayeb, Leena Elsadek et al. "Captive Labor: Exploitation of Incarcerated Workers." (2022). uchicago.edu

Massie, M. "Locked Up and Trafficked Out: Prison Labor and the Thirteenth Amendment." U. St. Thomas LJ (2023). [HTML]

Bamieh, Ryanne. "The New Abolition: The Legal Consequences of Ending All Slavery and Involuntary Servitude." Harvard Civil Rights-Civil Liberties Law Review (CR-CL) 59, no. 1 (2023). harvard.edu

Junaid, W. "Forced Prison Labor: Punishment for a Crime?." Nw. UL Rev. (2021). northwestern.edu

Smith, Sandra Susan, and Jonathan Simon. "Exclusion and extraction: Criminal justice contact and the reallocation of labor." RSF: The Russell Sage Foundation Journal of the Social Sciences 6, no. 1 (2020): 1-27. rsfjournal.org

Schenwar, M. "Prison by any other name: The harmful consequences of popular reforms." (2021). [HTML]

Woods, Tryon P. "The Police Power of Finance, Technology, Housing, and Education." In Pandemic Police Power, Public Health and the Abolition Question, pp. 87-108. Cham: Springer International Publishing, 2022. [HTML]

De Coninck, D. and Swinnen, M. "Exploring the news media-dark personality nexus: Linking television news consumption, the Dark Triad, and perceived refugee threat." Current Psychology (2023). springer.com

Tomes, N. "A "Creation of the Media" AIDS, Sensationalism, and Media Portrayals of Epidemic Risk." Feminist Media Histories (2022). [HTML]

MAGNONI, C. "CROSS-MEDIA AND TRANS-MEDIA STORYTELLING TO INCREASE THE AUDIENCE. THE CASE OF MIGRATION BETWEEN TRADITIONAL MEDIA AND ...." CLAUDIA ANAMARIA IOV (Ed.) . researchgate.net

Benekos, P. J. and Merlo, A. V. "Three strikes and you're out!: The political sentencing game." The American Court System (2020). [HTML]

Baumgartner, Frank R., Tamira Daniely, Kalley Huang, Sydney Johnson, Alexander Love, Lyle May, Patrice Mcgloin, Allison Swagert, Niharika Vattikonda, and Kamryn Washington. "Throwing away the key: the unintended consequences of "tough-on-crime" laws." Perspectives on Politics 19, no. 4 (2021): 1233-1246. unc.edu

Didwania, S. H. "Redundant leniency and redundant punishment in prosecutorial reforms." Okla. L. Rev. (2022). ou.edu

Clair, M. "Privilege and punishment: How race and class matter in criminal court." (2020). rutgers.edu

Amaker, J., Lyn, D. M., and Robertson, M. "Mass Incarceration & The Minority Vote: The Case for a Federal Ban on Felon Disenfranchisement." Notre Dame JL Ethics & Pub. Pol'y (2022). [HTML]

Jordan, K. A. "Critical race theory, wrongful convictions and disparate exonerations of minority and White youths in the United States.." Journal of Mental Health & Social Behavior (2021). gexinonline.com

Feigenberg, B. and Miller, C. "Racial divisions and criminal justice: Evidence from southern state courts." American Economic Journal: Economic Policy (2021). aeaweb.org

Light, M. T. "The declining significance of race in criminal sentencing: Evidence from US federal courts." Social Forces (2022). [HTML]

Oritseweyinmi Joe, I. "Structuring the public defender." IowA L. REv. (2020). uiowa.edu

Baćak, V., Lageson, S. E., and Powell, K. "The stress of injustice: public defenders and the frontline of American inequality." Social Forces (2024). defensenet.org

Green, B. A. and Roiphe, R. "When prosecutors politick: Progressive law enforcers then and now." J. Crim. L. & Criminology (2020). nyls.edu

Frame, G. "Some Men Just Want to Watch the World Burn." A Critical Companion to Christopher Nolan (2023). [HTML]

Klement, J. "Geo-economics: The interplay between geopolitics, economics, and investments." (2021). [HTML]

Caspi, A. "Overworking Public Defenders." Available at SSRN 4401227 (2023). [HTML]

Harris, H. M. "Building holistic defense: The design and evaluation of a social work centric model of public defense." Criminal Justice Policy Review (2020). [HTML]

Anwar, S., Bushway, S., and Engberg, J. "The impact of defense counsel at bail hearings." Science Advances (2023). science.org

Klauzner, I. and Yeong, S. "The impact of the Early Appropriate Guilty Plea reforms on guilty pleas, time to justice, and District Court finalisations." Crime and Justice Bulletin (2021). nsw.gov.au

Norris, Robert J., James R. Acker, Catherine L. Bonventre, and Allison D. Redlich. "Thirty years of innocence: Wrongful convictions and exonerations in the United States, 1989-2018." Wrongful Conv. L. Rev. 1 (2020): 2. wclawr.org

Carl, A. E. "Dead wrong: Capital punishment, wrongful convictions, and serious mental illness." Wrongful Conv. L. Rev. (2020). wclawr.org

Weintraub, J. N. and Bernstein, K. M. "Identifying and charging true perpetrators in cases of wrongful convictions." Wrongful Conv. L. Rev. (2020). wclawr.org

Gross, Samuel R., Maurice Possley, Kaitlin Roll, and Klara Stephens. "Government misconduct and convicting the innocent, the role of prosecutors, police and other law enforcement." U of Michigan Public Law Research Paper 21-003 (2020): 21-003. umich.edu

Gould, Jon B., Victoria M. Smiegocki, and Richard A. Leo. "Theorizing failed prosecutions." The Journal of Criminal Law and Criminology (1973-) 112, no. 2 (2022): 329-367. northwestern.edu

Goswami, G. K., and Aditi Goswami. "Forensic DNA in exonerations." In Handbook of DNA Forensic Applications and Interpretation, pp. 103-117. Singapore: Springer Nature Singapore, 2022. [HTML]

SCHETTERS, R., READER, S., and ADAMS, S. "Wrongful Convictions and Restoring the Rights of the Innocent." (2021). uvt.nl

Hession, F. M. "Constructing Guilt, Obstructing Truth: How the Spectacle of Wrongful Conviction Reveals and Magnifies Fundamental Flaws in the Criminal Justice System." (2020). bard.edu

Gudjonsson, G. H. "The science-based pathways to understanding false confessions and wrongful convictions." Frontiers in Psychology (2021). frontiersin.org

Norris, Robert J., Jennifer N. Weintraub, James R. Acker, Allison D. Redlich, and Catherine L. Bonventre. "The criminal costs of wrongful convictions: Can we reduce crime by protecting the innocent?." Criminology & Public Policy 19, no. 2 (2020): 367-388. researchgate.net

Martin, B. "Litigating Innocence: Why Systemic Reforms Are Needed to Exonerate, Pro Se Individuals." Law & Ineq. (2023). umn.edu

Patel, P., Zuhour, L., and McDermott, A. "Introduction to DNA in the Criminal Justice System." Voices of Forensic Science (2021). utoronto.ca

Saber, M., Nodeland, B., and Wall, R. "Exonerating DNA evidence in overturned convictions: analysis of data obtained from the National Registry of Exonerations." Criminal justice policy review (2022). [HTML]

Meintjes-Van der Walt, Lirieka, and Priviledge Dhliwayo. "DNA Evidence as the Basis for Conviction." Potchefstroom Electronic Law Journal/Potchefstroomse Elektroniese Regsblad 24, no. 1 (2021). ajol.info

Bellin, J. "The evidence rules that convict the innocent." Cornell L. Rev. (2020). wm.edu

Bechky, B. A. "Blood, powder, and residue: How crime labs translate evidence into proof." (2021). [HTML]

Dybdahl, T. L. "When innocence is not enough: hidden evidence and the failed promise of the Brady Rule." (2023). [HTML]

Ryan Sr, S. G. H. "Until I could be sure: How I stopped the death penalty in Illinois." (2020). [HTML]

Keys, Robin-Renee. "Exonerated, Yet Still Proving Innocence; The Fight For Wrongful Conviction Compensation in Louisiana." Southern University Law Center, Journal Of Race, Gender, & Poverty, Forthcoming (2021). racegenderpoverty.org

Bright, S. and Kwak, J. "The Fear of Too Much Justice: Race, Poverty, and the Persistence of Inequality in the Criminal Courts." (2023). [HTML]

Packrone, Seth E. "Educational Death Sentences: Addressing The Plight of Students With Disabilities in Adult Jails And Prisons." Harvard Civil Rights-Civil Liberties Law Review 59, no. 1 (2024). harvard.edu

Burke, R. "Deadly Decisions: Prosecutorial Misconduct and Prosecutorial Discretion in the Death Penalty System." U. Miami Race & Soc. Just. L. Rev. (2023). miami.edu

Sterling, R. W. "Invisible injustice: A review of punishment without crime: How our massive misdemeanor system traps the innocent and makes america more unequal by Alexandra ...." Journal of Community Psychology (2020). [HTML]

Rakoff, J. J. S. "Why the Innocent Plead Guilty and the Guilty Go Free: And Other Paradoxes of Our Broken Legal System." (2021). [HTML]

Messenger, T. "Profit and punishment: How America criminalizes the poor in the name of justice." (2021). [HTML]

Messmore, A. J. "Incarceration Rates and the Evolution of Anti-Drug Policy in the United States: Is Incarceration the Answer?." Am. J. Trial Advoc. (2020). [HTML]

Durose, Matthew R., and Leonardo Antenangeli. "Recidivism of prisoners released in 34 states in 2012: A 5-year follow-up period (2012–2017)." Washington, DC: Bureau of Justice Statistics (2021). antoniocasella. eu

Heimer, Karen, Sarah E. Malone, and Stacy De Coster. "Trends in women's incarceration rates in US prisons and jails: A tale of inequalities." Annual review of criminology 6 (2023): 85-106. annualreviews.org

Cochran, Joshua C., Elisa L. Toman, Ryan T. Shields, and Daniel P. Mears. "A uniquely punitive turn? Sex offenders and the persistence of punitive sanctioning." Journal of Research in Crime and Delinquency 58, no. 1 (2021): 74-118. sagepub.com

Bailey, S. "Alternatives to Incarceration: Reducing Recidivism Among Nonviolent Offenders Through Post-Incarceration Resources." (2022). [HTML]

Razali, Arafat, Jamaludin Mustaffa, and Siti Rozaina Kamsani. "Reducing recidivism among former offenders: Strategies to increase success in social reintegration." Turkish Online Journal of Qualitative Inquiry 12, no. 3 (2021). [HTML]

WALKER, S. D. "Beyond Incarceration: Identification of Post-Incarceration Strategies for Successful Reintegration." (2024). waldenu.edu

Klein Haneveld, E. L. M. "Individual differences in the treatment of psychopathic offenders." (2022). uva.nl

Kaeble, D. and Alper, M. "Probation and parole in the United States, 2017–2018." Bureau of Justice Statistics (2020). oup.com

Robson, Sarah, Julia A. Yesberg, Marc S. Wilson, and Devon LL Polaschek. "A fresh start or the devil, you know? Examining relationships between release location choices, community experiences, and recidivism for high-risk parolees." International journal of offender therapy and comparative criminology 64, no. 6-7 (2020): 635-653. ucl.ac.uk

Wiggins, Benjamin, Edward E. Rhine, Bree Crye, Robin Tu, and Kelly Lyn Mitchell. "Parole Rules in the United States: Conditions of Parole in Historical Perspective, 1956–2020." Criminal Justice Review 47, no. 2 (2022): 185-207. umn.edu

Sabriseilabi, S., Williams, J., and Sadri, M. "How does race moderate the effect of religion dimensions on attitudes toward the death penalty?." Societies (2022). mdpi.com

Itskovich, E., Factor, R., and Ohana, D. "Haven't they suffered enough? Time to exoneration following wrongful conviction of racially marginalized minority-vs. majority-group members." Punishment & Society (2023). sagepub.com

Westbrook, L. "The matrix of violence: Intersectionality and necropolitics in the murder of transgender people in the United States, 1990–2019." Gender & Society (2023). [HTML]

www.ingramcontent.com/pod-product-compliance
Lightning Source LLC
LaVergne TN
LVHW010113170826
845678LV00012B/2385
* 9 7 9 8 3 3 0 2 5 7 2 8 7 *